D0627280

Rural Reminiscences

THE AGONY OF SURVIVAL

Kenneth Hassebrock

Rural Reminiscences

THE AGONY OF SURVIVAL

Iowa State University Press / Ames

Kenneth Hassebrock grew up on three different farms in northern Iowa during the 1920s and 1930s. After serving in World War II, he became a civil engineer. Now retired, he lives in Sacramento, California.

© 1990 Iowa State University Press, Ames, Iowa 50010
All rights reserved

Manufactured in the United States of America
⊛ This book is printed on acid-free paper.

No part of this book may be reproduced in any form or by any electronic or mechanical means, including information storage and retrieval systems, without written permission from the publisher, except for brief passages quoted in a review.

First edition, 1990

Library of Congress Cataloging-in-Publication Data

Hassebrock, Kenneth.
    Rural reminiscences : the agony of survival / Kenneth Hassebrock.
  —1st ed.
    p. c.
    ISBN 0-8138-0284-9
    1. Farm life—Iowa—History—20th century. 2. Iowa—Social life and customs. 3. Iowa—Rural conditions. 4. Hassebrock, Kenneth—Childhood and youth. 5. Iowa—Biography. I. Title.
F621.H29 1990
977.7′009734—dc20   90-33656

To my parents . . .

*and all those whose survival
required an uncommon devotion
to the principle of self-help*

Contents

Preface

An old crusty individual once told me that the subject of farming was about as interesting as a "dose of salts." Such, no doubt, is the thinking of many, especially those tired of hearing a monotonous repetition of how hard life was in "the good old days." Most still see "the hick with the stick" in Grant Wood's *American Gothic,* which shows a rural dude, pitchfork in hand, standing beside his humble companion.

While this viewpoint is not uncommon, it is interesting to note that ranching occupies a more favorable spot in the emotional heart of the general public. (The individual noted above was a great admirer of Westerns.) This is due, in part, to the use of the horse as a means of transportation instead of a source of power for heavy pulling. The cowboy is held in high esteem—the physical caressing of one's rear end while riding a horse appears to mentally massage a person into a hypnotic state, while draft horses remind one of hard, physical labor obtained only under the lashes of a whip (unless pulling a beer wagon, of course).

While the popularity of farming may leave something to be desired, those who lived in this environment led lives as real, as poignant, and yes, as important as those in other fields of human endeavor—including ranching. A few of us were fortunate enough to have witnessed and to have played a part in this activity during the 1920s and 1930s when farming began its first serious transformation from an extensively diversified animal-powered operation, requiring a tremendous amount of backbreaking physical labor, to a highly mechanized scientifically oriented business, requiring little physical but substantially more mental effort; a time when horsepower "under the hood" began to rapidly replace that "on the hoof"; a time when a man's role as virtually a beast of burden was greatly reduced and the need for a son to assist the family until he was twenty-one became less important. Of course this change was not without its price.

It has been said that there is an ebb and flow to the course of human events, a cycle in human affairs where to some much is given and from others much required. If such be the case, most would surely say that my generation experienced an ebb tide. Iowa farmers had experienced fluctuating economic conditions during the 1920s and as the 1930s approached, signs of distress began to appear. As fate would have it, the stock market crash in October of 1929 came seven months after my parents moved onto their own farm, and as the Great Depression approached, they found the burden of carrying their mortgage increasingly difficult to bear. They lost the farm in 1931 and our lives were then tempered in the crucible of the depression and honed by the hardness of adversity.

The Great Depression has received substantial publicity, but since it literally controlled our lives during the period noted in Part Two and Part Three of this volume, the repetition of a few pertinent facts concerning this debacle is in order.

The prices we received for our commodities dropped to as low as $2.54 per hundredweight for steers, $2.25 per hundredweight for hogs, $0.16 per pound for butterfat, $0.08 a dozen for eggs, and $0.10 a bushel for corn. (Some farmers did not take the time to shell corn kernels from the cob before burning them in the stove.) Farmers were used to fluctuating financial conditions and at first their criticism of government was the usual muted kind, but as the years progressed and the depression deepened, it became more biting. A few used expressions no less intense than those used later during the Vietnam War, and although I did not hear anyone advocating the breaking of any law or see anyone doing so, newspaper reports indicated that some of this was taking place (stopping milk trucks and dumping their contents, etc.).

Rural opinion had its effect on politics and after the Roosevelt administration took office in March of 1933, farm programs were introduced to assist farmers in their financial difficulties. First reactions to these programs were mixed. To maintain prices at a reasonable level, production had to be controlled and this meant acreage limitations on crops (the intent was to have an ever-normal granary) and the killing of little pigs. Production limitations at a time when some people were going hungry were not understood and were opposed. Participation in the program was voluntary, but those who did not join were not guaranteed a minimum price for their commodities. Although criticism of these programs was extensive, many, if not most, of the farmers joined, and sealed corn (and other support programs) soon became a part of U.S. agriculture. (If you were in the program, you could "seal" some of your corn in an adequate crib and obtain some of the guaranteed price before it was shelled and sent to market.)

Obviously, our reduced income affected my life. At no time did I ever have an allowance; I literally lived without money except for a few coins received on Saturday night or special occasions. Instilled in me was a "do-it-yourself" philosophy where debt was a quagmire to be approached with caution. I acquired traits of frugality that were never to leave me, even when circumstances made them frivolous.

All lives are unique and mine was no less so than others, but the experiences noted herein provide a realistic glimpse of life as it was then lived by the male side of the family on the farm. (I believe it self-evident that the woman's role was of equal importance, but it quickly became apparent that the reporting of the female role had to lie in more capable hands than mine, and only brief references are made thereto.) Life involves countless experiences, most of which are forgotten, a few selectively remembered, and these clouded by prejudice and vanity, but an authentic picture of a way of life demands the inclusion of our deficiencies, and this, within my limited ability, I have attempted to do. All of us have a rendezvous with destiny, and in our journey we move with the involuntary flow of evolutionary change, adapting to that which we must, improving that which we can. Our experiences, mundane though they appear at the time, are the ingredients from which history is made.

My perspective is one of time and distance, an overview of the forest instead of a microscopic examination of the bark on specific trees, of remembering the past but not being part of the present. My vocational agriculture class exposed me to a scientific future in farming, but the high tech operation of today, in which various biological and chemical agents are used to increase the production of flora and to expedite the transformation of flora into fauna, developed from but played no part in the events noted herein.

I was fortunate to have been a member of a family that had strong moral leadership and we lived, worked, and played together, sharing the agony and the ecstasy of bittersweet times. Whatever merit this record contains is due in large part to my brother, Wilbur, and my sister, Anna Marie. Dad, Mother, and Dolores are now with us only in spirit but their contribution is self-evident; their direct guidance has been sorely missed. Obviously my efforts would have been in vain without the complete and loyal support of my wife, Mildred. Her background on an Iowa farm near Le Mars did not differ greatly from mine and her unwavering encouragement and assistance proved to be the catalyst without which this kind of effort would be impossible. My debt to those who have enriched my memories and assisted me in my endeavors obviously includes countless others, any listing of which would be incomplete and will therefore not be attempted. However, prominent on such a list would be Claire Torgersen, who faithfully and with the highest degree of fidelity transcribed my hieroglyphics into magnetic properties so vital to that indispensable writing tool—the word processor.

The distance I have traveled on the road to that unobtainable goal—perfection—has been insufficient to reduce the number of errors herein to insignificance. These, and other deficiencies, are mine and mine alone; deliberate they are not but they are limited, I hope, in scope.

Rural Reminiscences

THE AGONY OF SURVIVAL

Introduction

The pioneer's inevitable quest for gain fueled the westward expansion of farms and ranches in the United States, encouraging immigration and thereby embedding more deeply European ancestral roots into the fertile soil of our nation. My roots thread their way from northern Germany to Iowa during the latter part of the nineteenth century and the first few decades of the twentieth century.

The area in what is now Iowa had in excess of forty thousand inhabitants when John C. Fremont was briefly involved in its surveys in 1841, and their numbers increased to nearly two hundred thousand by 1850, but extensive settlement had to await the development of a practical means of getting farm products to distant urban markets. The typical family-size farm was considered to be 160 acres (a quarter section) and access to it was over crude, unimproved dirt roads located on the one-mile grid used in laying out the typical six-mile-square townships. (Although forty acres and a mule may have been considered an adequate farm operation in some sections of our country, in Iowa it was 160 acres, which was in conformity with the Homestead Act of 1862. The land was subdivided into townships and ranges following the Federal Land Ordinance of 1785.) Cattle had to be driven to local markets and other transportation required the use of horses. Thus, an extensive rail network, with towns located a few miles apart, was a prerequisite for the surge of immigration that followed. Much of this was to take place in the latter half of the nineteenth century when my grandparents came to the United

States and eventually settled on farms in Hamilton County in north-central Iowa.

The desire to be with one's own kind led to ethnic communities in which the language in general use was that of the old country. Our grandparents spoke Low German and even though they required a sufficient degree of expertise in the use of English to communicate with others, the native language was the one used at home and with most outside contacts. (The official language of Germany was known as High German and it was the one used by ministers when giving sermons in German. It differed substantially from Low German and most of the grandchildren could not understand it.) Although my parents were educated in public schools in this country where English was the only language permitted, the use of German was so ingrained that it continued to be the language used in our home.

Mother's parents lived on a farm northeast of Kamrar, a small town in Hamilton County, where her education consisted of eight years in a local rural school. She then worked as a clerk in a store in Kamrar before her marriage to Dad.

Dad's parents lived on a farm southeast of Kamrar (their address was Jewell, Iowa), where he too attended a rural school. A desire to continue his education then led him to take classes at the Dubuque German College and Seminary in Dubuque, Iowa, from 1907 to 1910. (The name of the institution was changed to the University of Dubuque in 1919.) After leaving Dubuque, he enrolled in a mechanics school in Des Moines, but fire destroyed the school soon after his arrival and he returned home.

After their marriage in 1912 my parents lived in Kamrar where Dad operated a hardware-implement-car sales business in which his father, George Hassebrock, had an interest. Wilbur, the first addition to our family, was born in Webster City Hospital in June of 1914 while they were living in this community.

In 1916 grandfather sold his interest in this business and purchased a two hundred-acre farm two miles north and one and a third miles east of Germania, Iowa (changed to Lakota during World War I), in Kossuth County in northern Iowa. My parents then moved to this farm and began their farming career.

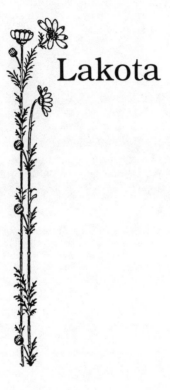

Lakota

*The Dubuque German College and Seminary band,
Dubuque, Iowa, circa 1910. Dad is fifth from the left,
second row from the top. The man on his left is Otto
Frerking, who became our pastor at Lakota.*

*Lakota house, 1928. The brooder house is on the left
and the garage is on the right.*

Lakota barn, 1928.

Lakota corncrib and oats bin, 1927. A small portion of the chicken house and the hog house appears on the left. Our hand cornsheller stands in front of the corncrib, our buggy in front of the oats bin, and our corn picker between the two buildings.

Students at the Lakota rural school, circa 1928. Kenneth is on the left in the front row shielding his eyes. Dolores is second from the right in the front row.

Dolores, Anna Marie, and the Whippet, 1928. Our Lakota house is in the background.

Wilbur, the buggy, and interested passengers, 1928.
Wilbur is third from the left in the rear. Kenneth is
directly in front of him.

A 1919 Hart Parr tractor. This is the model we had. The
angle-iron lugs on the rear wheels and the sharp rims
on the front wheels were removed from this tractor so
that it could be driven on hard-surfaced roads.

Hay stacker. Many of the components of this old stacker are made of steel; ours, however, was mostly wood.

Buck rake. This buck rake differs from the one we had in several respects: our horses walked alongside the horizontal tines, one on each side; the seat was located on a cantilever projecting from the rear of the rake; and the wheels were near the rear of the fork, not under the seat as shown here.

A modified McCormick Deering corn picker, circa 1927. Henry Siebels of Le Mars, Iowa, is shown sitting on a picker he modified and powered with a Model T Ford engine. This modification differed from ours, which had an engine mounted on the right side.

Farm, Town, and Transportation

THE FARM

Memories have an indelible quality that time distorts but cannot erase, and images are embellished thereby. Such is the case with my recollections of the Lakota farm. It was home for my parents from 1916 to 1929, where my brother grew to be a teenager and where my sisters and I were born (Dolores 1919, Kenneth 1921, Anna Marie 1927). Age limited my role to that of a juvenile observer, unsaddled with responsibilities and viewing activities that would soon retreat from reality into history. Such a detached innocence tends to inspire a romantic perspective quite unlike that of an active participant.

Although the farm's improvements were not the newest or best, affluence was in evidence. It possessed a full complement of buildings, including a modest house, barn, hog house, chicken house, corncrib, oats bin, garage (former stable), brooder house, and pump house. It was bordered on the south by an unimproved dirt road and on the west by a dredge ditch. (Iowa prairie soil was very fertile but much of it was poorly drained. To remedy this condition, dredges were used to deepen the natural drainage courses, and adjacent farmers drained their land to these ditches by using clay tile embedded in the soil a few feet below the surface of the ground.) The farmyard was adjacent to the road and surrounded by trees, including a large orchard on the southeast corner. A one-room schoolhouse was located on one acre of ground immediately west of the yard.

THE TOWN

Lakota was a typical small Iowa town of the early 1900s with a population of a few hundred. It had gravel streets (they were paved in the 1930s), and there were hitching posts in front of many of its stores. Its railroad facilities included a depot and an elevated, wood-staved water tank used to replenish the water supply in engine tenders. Trading facilities included a grain elevator, lumberyard, hardware store, drugstore, gas station, two grocery stores (one sold dry goods), a creamery (called the Germania Creamery), and a Ford dealership that sold tractors as well as cars. There were a number of churches, including the Presbyterian one that we attended. A water tower provided storage and pressure for its water supply. Each facility had to provide for the disposal of its own waste.

Local towns were not only terminals for travel and transportation, they were also the only urban environment available on a regular basis to isolated rural residents. (County seats were generally larger, but in our case, Algona, our county seat, was thirty miles from our farm, which meant we seldom traveled to it.) My experiences with electric lights, running water, and flush toilets were limited to those at church and an occasional visit to a friend's home in town.

ROADS

The umbilical cords that tied farms to towns consisted of roads, many of which appeared to have evolved little since the formation of trails by man or beast. Most were dirt, although the main roads between towns were being graveled. Our access to Lakota was over a dirt road, one and one-third miles west and then two miles south on a gravel road (now U.S. 169).

Dirt roads were made by using a grader to move soil from adjacent ground, which formed a ditch, and placing it on a grade where drainage was expedited and where snow was less likely to accumulate. A neighbor was hired by the county to periodically go over the road with a horse-drawn grader to fill the ruts and smooth the surface. There was no snowplow service and when deep drifts formed, adjacent farmers had to shovel a lane through them by hand.

The placement of gravel on the surface of a dirt road increases its strength when wet, resulting in a firmer support for vehicles. Roads were being graveled as finances permitted, using numerous conveniently located gravel pits. (These glacial deposits were not plentiful in all rural areas; the glaciers did not encroach into southern Iowa.) Unfortunately, this process was slow and getting the farmer out of the mud was not to be substantially accomplished until the advent of federal farm-to-market road programs later in the 1930s.

Farmers obtained money for daily living expenses from the sale of cream and eggs, and lack of refrigeration dictated their rapid transit to market during warm weather. As a result, three trips were made to town each week for this purpose, and in our case, two additional ones on Sunday for our mandatory church attendance. Cars were the preferred means of doing so but the transition from horsepower in the flesh to horsepower under the hood was still taking place and horse-drawn vehicles were not uncommon.

HORSE-DRAWN VEHICLES

In the spring, when their surface was thawing and the frost below had not yet disappeared, and in the summer during heavy rains, dirt roads became quagmires where the wheels of vehicles sought firm support deep under the soft mud. The most efficient wheel for doing so was large in diameter and narrow in width. Although it used horses, and was therefore very slow moving, the lightweight buggy was the best vehicle available for the transportation of personnel on muddy roads. Its large-diameter wheels sank into the mud to relatively firm soil and their narrow widths created small ruts, permitting a horse to continue forward movement without excessive effort. We had a buggy and I understood it had seen frequent action in the past, but I seldom recall its use except by my brother, Wilbur, as a recreational vehicle.

Wagons were used to move crops and materials about the farm and to transport items to town. They were designed for the most convenient operation. We had two wagons, one with large-diameter wheels with narrow rims, which were better for use in mud, and the other with smaller diameter but wider wheels and a wagon box that sat closer to the ground for easy loading. We had two triple boxes, one for each wagon. (A triple wagon box had three side boards, each holding twelve bushels of ear corn when level full, one bushel for each inch of depth. The two top boards could be easily removed making a single or double box.) Dad had purchased these wagons when he closed out his store at Kamrar and his name, as the dealer, was printed on the sides.

In the winter, cutters were good for use in snow of moderate depths, but they had the same limitations all sleighs have—a horse cannot pull them through deep snow; they cannot be backed up; and when snow begins to melt, patches of mud appear, making transit difficult. We had a cutter but its condition had deteriorated to the point where it was no longer used for family transportation; it too was consigned to those seeking recreational pursuits.

The bobsled was made to support a wagon box or hayrack, and when transporting personnel, a triple wagon box was generally used. Their runners were made of wood and they were low in profile, locating the wagon box closer to the ground than a wagon chassis. Runners had steel strips attached to their sliding surfaces to reduce wear. Although not common, ours had a longitudinal groove in these straps to reduce the tendency of the runners to slide sideways. There were no seats, so all riders had to stand and hang on to the sides when the vehicle was in motion.

Since the weather was always cold when sleighs were in use, warm clothing was the norm, but the wagon box severely limited physical activity and with the cold air freely circulating around our bodies, we soon became chilled to the bone. We then made a robotlike exit at our destination as stiff leg muscles slowly removed the cramps that bound them. Brief sleigh rides with desirable companions under ideal conditions are one thing; when made out of necessity and under adverse conditions, they are something else. Let those who have not indulged in this activity continue to enjoy their dreams of playing Santa in a winter wonderland.

The use of horses for transportation had its obvious drawbacks. Carriage horses moved at a faster pace than glacially slow draft horses, but they too were very slow compared to motorized vehicles. By the 1920s, most farmers kept only draft horses and they were only used to go to town when necessity dictated.

Speed was not the only deterrent to the use of horses. Under certain conditions, they could and did panic and a runaway resulted. During a runaway the driver is not in control; he or she can only encourage the horses to follow a nondestructive path until they exhaust themselves, ending up completely covered with lathered sweat. Obviously this can be a very frightening and dangerous experience.

AUTOMOBILES

Although their performance left much to be desired and maintenance was a problem, the advantages possessed by the automobile made its acquisition by farmers popular. At first cars were only used when road conditions were good. Although it was not unusual for a farmer to put the car on blocks in the passageway of the corncrib during the winter, car transportation soon increased, even under adverse and winter road conditions.

Gravel roads were usually passable, but travel was not necessarily pleasant. They immediately developed a washboard-type surface with ridges strategically spaced to provide maximum impact at cruising speed. These bumps subjected the vehicle and its contents to a rapid up-and-down motion at a frequency uniquely in phase with that which induces a maximum impact on the rear end. In dry weather, clouds of dust were generated by fast moving vehicles, and because the treads of tires were conveniently spaced to pick up small stones and heave them directly at passing vehicles, occupants were advised to protect themselves from a meteor shower of unprecedented proportions. The windshields of many cars could be opened or laid down in a horizontal position and when so placed, the full sandblasting effect would be experienced. An occasional larger stone added an element of danger to those sitting in the front seat, enhancing the thrill they were then experiencing. (Windshields did not entirely eliminate this danger; shatterproof laminated safety glass was not yet in use.)

For most farmers, access to town was over roads that included a stretch of unimproved dirt and these roads provided the setting for experiences that added little to the serenity of life. Before the introduction of the balloon tire in the 1920s, car wheels were quite large in diameter and narrow in width but the much heavier car and the use of its wheels to propel it resulted in its becoming stuck in mud and snow much easier than the buggy. This problem did not cease with the use of balloon tires—

in fact, it became more acute. The balloon tire used a lower air pressure to provide a more comfortable ride, but its size had to be increased to do so and the wheel diameter was generally reduced in the process. These tires had a tendency to become wedged in previously made narrow ruts and axles were then closer to the ground where intimate contact took place more frequently.

Chains were in common use but their installation was frequently delayed until actually needed. Since the natural course of human events dictated that the act of getting stuck be reserved for those trips where all passengers were dressed in their Sunday clothes, when Dad went wading through the mud to put on chains, he did so in high style.

Getting a chain completely around a wheel that is up to its axle in mud was no easy task; doing so, and attaching the inside snap connector without accumulating mud on knees and sleeves required a degree of expertise few possessed. The operation was obviously not conducive to the enhancement of religious fervor, and even when accomplished successfully, the ordeal was not necessarily over. In all probability, the axle and the ground had developed a sufficient degree of intimacy, which meant they refused to part. Chains were then of little use.

When this happened, the standard operating procedure was for the driver to make a reconnaissance of the immediate vicinity to see if there were any fence posts, tree limbs, brush, straw, or miscellaneous fiber that could be used to provide sufficient support for the recalcitrant wheel. If the materials available proved to be inadequate, it was necessary to go to an adjacent farmer and have him harness up a team to get us out.

Because of its price the Model T Ford was no doubt the most popular car. However, there was no shortage of other makes and models. The folks had had a Maxwell when they lived at Kamrar, but changed to Chevrolets when they lived at Lakota. The first one I recall was a 1921 touring model.

The most distinguishing feature of this car, as far as I was concerned, was its snap-on side curtains containing small isinglass (mica) windows. These curtains, used during cold, inclement weather, severely limited the view, and the aerodynamic features of the vehicle were such that they did little to prevent the entry of a continuous blast of subzero arctic air in the winter. The chilly, dark environment within made one feel entombed. The buffalo robe kept our lower extremities at a temperature just high enough to maintain circulation in our legs, but not in our toes, and the loss of sensation would continue for some time after our entry into a warm room.

Automobile improvements did not go unnoticed; the purchase of a new car soon became a status symbol for the upwardly mobile. Some dealers went directly to the farms to talk to prospective customers and this was the case with the Whippet salesman who lived at Ledyard. His first appearance on our farm was on a Sunday and Dad quickly informed him that he did no business on that day. The salesman returned later in the week and bargaining began.

Shortly thereafter, we became the proud possessors of a modern car, one which was glass enclosed, had four-wheel brakes and balloon tires. The windows provided substantially more visibility than snap-on curtains and their weather tightness resulted in a more comfortable interior environment. Although there was no heater, when the robe was used (back seat only), riding became bearable in cold weather.

As previously noted, the surfaces of main highways left much to be desired and speeds in excess of forty-five miles per hour were not recommended. However, this did not discourage the use of cars for trips of moderate length. We made at least one trip a year to see our relatives at Kamrar, approximately one hundred miles each way.

Trips of this length required advance preparations. Mechanical problems were common and fixing flats alongside the road was part of the cost of operating a car; no one ventured far from home without adequate tools, including a jack, tire pump, tire irons, and a tube repair kit. (Many cars had a tool kit attached to the running board.) On long trips, it was wise to take additional oil and water for the car.

These trips also required advance preparations on Mother's part. Eating in restaurants was unknown and a picnic lunch was a must. These lunches were eaten at picnic tables when available, but on our trips to Kamrar, which were usually made during the summer, Dad would seek out a rural school and we would use its grounds for a park.

Unfortunately, because they did not have trunks, it was difficult to transport farm commodities. However, most farmers used their cars for this purpose, as well as for transporting people. Our fifteen- and thirty-dozen egg cases could be put on the seats, but

full cream cans presented a problem. Dad solved it by construct-
ing a wooden box and attaching it temporarily to the rear of the
car when taking cream to town.

The speed of a car or truck, even at fifteen to twenty-five
miles per hour, was much greater than that of a horse and
farmers soon sought their use for bringing all their commodities
to town. Truckers were occasionally hired, especially for the ship-
ment of cattle, but the purchase of such a vehicle was beyond the
means of most farmers. For convenience, and to save money,
cars were put to use towing a wagon or trailer.

Wagons were not built to exceed the speed of a horse and this
precluded their use except for very short trips. It soon became
apparent that a rubber-tired vehicle was a necessity, which led to
the development of four-wheeled trailers.

I do not recall any commercially built trailers in use at that
time; those I saw were all homemade affairs composed of crudely
assembled old auto parts. Dad used the chassis of a 1918 Chevrolet car he had junked to make our four-wheeler, and used a
wagon box for its body.

The construction of a four-wheeled trailer having no undesirable trailing characteristics at any speed was a task beyond the
capabilities of most farmers and, as noted on page 155, most of
them had to be towed at a low speed.

TRAINS

The building of railroads in Iowa began in the 1850s
with the extension of those going west from Chicago. A compre-
hensive network would be completed throughout the state
during the next thirty years. (The planning and construction of
the transcontinental railroad—completed in 1869—played a part
in the location of main lines through Iowa.) Trains were still the
primary means of long-distance travel for both passengers and
freight in the 1920s and 1930s and their importance to farm
communities should not be underestimated. (Fast, transcontinental passenger trains were not in evidence at Lakota and
Ledyard. My familiarity with them was to take place later at
Manly.) Freight trains were used to ship grain, livestock, and
farm machinery, while express packages and mail were transported in special cars attached to passenger trains. Passenger

trains operated on a firm schedule and therefore had priority. Special trains were used to move livestock long distances to packing plants near large urban centers. These trains also had a high priority since federal law stated that livestock could only remain on board without food or water a specified length of time. Freight was paid for to a railhead and facilities for loading and unloading livestock, heavy machinery, and grain were available at all towns. (The name "elevator" for the storage of grain was apparently derived from the fact that grain was stored at higher elevations in adjacent storage buildings so that gravity could be used to move it into the railcars by means of chutes.)

The Rock Island line served Lakota, while Ledyard, a few miles northwest, was on the Chicago and Northwestern (CNW). The CNW also went through Kamrar and it was this line that encouraged movement of farmers from the vicinity of Hamilton County to Kossuth County after its extension to Ledyard in the 1880s. (It was also of great importance to us since it was the terminus of our train-traveling relatives.) Most communities had daily passenger service, but when passenger trains were not available, people rode in the çaboose of a freight train.

Train arrivals did not go unnoticed. The monstrous steam-snorting iron beast would signal its arrival with a blast or two from its whistle, and the ground seemed to shake as it slowly approached the depot with a ringing bell cautioning all to keep their distance.

Railroads were not only important to rural communities; they were also a necessity for large urban centers. It should be noted that they kept a substantial portion of our population employed; working on the railroad was a way of life for many. Mother had two brothers who were locomotive engineers, highly paid and sought after positions.

The One-Room School

Iowans have always strongly supported sufficient education to learn reading, writing, and arithmetic and in rural areas, one-room schools were located so that all students were within walking distance. As previously noted, our school was conveniently located adjacent to our farmyard. Its facilities, typical of most such schools, included the main building, a storage shed, outhouses for boys and girls, and a flag pole.

The main building was one room with a row of double desks along each side. The teacher's desk was at the front and a blackboard was on the wall behind her. A heating stove was located near the front and center of the room, and kerosene lamps were placed on supports along the wall. Two students sat at each desk and materials were stored in an open shelf under the desk top.

The only teacher I remember at this school was Eva Winters, a daughter of our neighbor across the road, who had finished high school and taken a normal school training course during the summer at Iowa State Teacher's College (now the University of Northern Iowa). Her task was obviously not an easy one. Not only did she have to teach eight different grade levels in the same room, but she also had to keep the school clean, bring a pail of water for drinking, and keep the school warm in winter. The latter task required lighting the stove early enough so that the room would be habitable when the students arrived.

Although I learned to read and write at this school, my academic achievements left much to be desired, due for the most part to my unscholarly attitude; studying held little interest for me. I recall Eva patiently assisting me in selecting the right words in a multiple choice test. Unfortunately, my unpleasant entry later into the Ledyard school leads me to believe her kind help might have been excessive. Competition with others at my level of achievement did not seem to exist and I proceeded at my own leisurely pace.

The harsh environment of a strict school master with a whip readily available at his side did not exist at this school. All the students knew Eva personally and friendly persuasion was the usual means of correcting less than admirable activities. I do not recall Eva using any accessories to enforce discipline, although physical force was not entirely unknown.

We did not have playground equipment, but our lack of familiarity with such recreational aids did not deter our participation in games of a juvenile nature. The noon hour and recesses are not remembered for their long duration.

The last day of school was always a happy occasion. Many mothers were present to see their dear ones compete in running and outdoor games and since all knew each other, it was a sociable affair. No doubt Eva found it difficult to hand out bad report cards—even my grades were of passing quality.

Upon the completion of eighth grade, students could take an exam given by the county. If the exam was successfully passed, students were permitted to enter the ninth grade at the Ledyard Consolidated School. This school, located approximately seven miles northwest of our farm, used buses to bring its students to school; however, they did not go past our farm and it was necessary for students living along our road to go to the Telkamp corner a mile west of our farm to catch the bus.

Standing along the side of a road in subzero weather waiting for a bus was not a great inducement to continue one's education and many students did not do so. Wilbur is one who did and he entered high school at Ledyard during the fall of 1928. Like all farm boys, he had chores to do before and after school, and since Dad was generally busy, it was necessary for him to walk to the Telkamp corner. There were also occasions, such as corn-picking time, when he had to stay home to help Dad for a week or two. From the standpoint of Wilbur's education, it was fortunate that we moved to a farm closer to Ledyard in March of 1929, where bus service was available.

Stackers, Puffers, and Pickers

Most of the farm operations I observed at Lakota were similar to those I actively participated in later at Ledyard, and they are, therefore, covered in that section, but those noted below were not. These operations also occupied a significant spot in the kaleidoscope of rural activities, and are set apart here because they are part of my Lakota memories.

THE HAY STACKER

The popular diversified farm of the 1920s grew extensive feed for its own use, and hay, being a significant part of the winter diet of horses and cattle, was one of its main crops. (When Ledyard first began to develop, it was occasionally referred to as the "hay capital.") In the beginning, when much of the ground was still unbroken prairie, farmers used native grasses for hay, but as this resource diminished, domestically grown plants such as timothy, clovers, and alfalfa replaced them.

Winters were long and severe and food and shelter were necessary for the survival of all farm animals during this period. Barns, built to shelter cattle and horses, included a second-story haymow for storage. Unfortunately, our haymow was not large enough to store all the hay our animals required and the surplus had to be placed in stacks outside.

The best place to stack hay for convenient use was in the

24

farmyard near the barn, but this required extensive hand labor during the hay-making process; because we did not have a loader, the hay had to be loaded on the rack by hand, transported to the yard, and unloaded by hand. Since other farm tasks also demanded extensive labor during this period, Dad expedited the process by using a hay stacker to stack the surplus hay in the field.

Our stacking equipment consisted of a stacker and a buck rake. The buck rake was, in effect, a large hay fork that was used to scoop up hay from the windrows formed in the field by the rake, and to move it directly to the stacker. The buck rake had a set of horizontal steel-tipped wooden tines that moved along the ground under the hay, which piled up against a set of vertical tines as the rake moved forward. The operator had a seat on a cantilever projection that extended to the rear where the operator's weight was used as a counterbalance, pivoting on two small wheels near the rear of the fork. (The seat was adjustable forward and backward for the weight of different operators.)

A horse was placed on each side of the rake, straddling the windrow and pulling the rake forward. When the rake was taking on hay, the operator would get off the seat to keep the horizontal tines on the ground where they would slide under the hay. However, when the buck rake was full, the operator would turn the horses from the windrow, get on the seat, and head for the stacker.

The stacker looked like a catapult, consisting of a large hay fork, similar to the buck rake, that was attached to two arms that pivoted about the base of the stacker frame. The frame projected up into the air, providing a stop for the lifter in the vertical position. The structure was mounted on wheels and moved about by a team of horses with the lifter in the vertical position. After being located at the desired site in the hay field, the stacker was firmly staked down for use.

The hay on the buck rake was deposited on the lifter fork while it was in a down position. The buck rake was moved into the lifter fork so that their horizontal tines meshed and the hay was firmly pressed against the vertical tines of the stacker fork. The buck rake operator got off the seat and backed the buck rake away from the stacker, leaving the hay deposited on the stacker fork.

The stacker operator used a team to raise the lifter by means of ropes and pulleys until the lifter arms had pivoted to slightly more than a ninety degree angle from the horizontal. At this point the lifter came against its frame, which stopped it and permitted the hay to slide off the slightly downward sloping rear tines onto the stack. The lifter was then lowered by pulling it back and slowly backing up the team. While the buck rake operator was getting another load of hay, the stacker operator moved the newly dropped hay about, shaping the stack.

Watching a stacker in operation was an exciting experience. Although light in weight, the load of hay was large in volume and as the catapult slowly rose, one had the feeling that the seemingly flimsy structure was straining excessively under the load and would collapse. It seemed to emit a sigh of relief as it dropped its load and to relax as it was slowly lowered into a reclining position. I maintained a considerable distance from this structure when this activity was taking place and I was seldom a lone observer. All within viewing distance would lock their eyes on the catapult until the cycle had been completed.

Stackers were not popular in Iowa because they could only be used in the hay field where the hay was readily accessible to the buck rake. For those who raised hay for sale, buyers found the stacks in the field as accessible as those in the farmyard. However, for those who kept all their hay for their own use as we did, the labor required for moving hay to consuming animals during inclement winter weather made the use of stackers and haystacks in the fields undesirable. Our stacker was disassembled for our move to Ledyard and was never used again.

THE STEAM ENGINE

The steam engine has its own unique nostalgic niche in the evolution of farming. It was the only source of power used for threshing in the early 1900s and was still in use in Dad's threshing ring in the latter 1920s. Although the threshing machine would remain with us for more than a decade, the steam engine's demise was apparent.

Originally called a separator, the threshing machine was a rather large machine that required extensive power for proper operation. During its early development, this power was provided by horses. Up to six teams were hitched to the end of booms that radiated from a large-diameter ring gear, frequently referred to as a turntable, that meshed with smaller gears. As the teams walked in circles, the gears transferred the power to the threshing machine through tumbling rods and universal joints. This method of powering the machine soon proved unacceptable and steam engines, then coming into use, quickly replaced the horse.

The first steam engines were not self-propelled but had to be moved about by horses. However, as their popularity increased, manufacturers geared the engines to a set of lugged wheels enabling the machines to move themselves with a threshing machine in tow.

In Dad's threshing ring, the threshing equipment (thresher, steam engine, and water wagon) was owned by Ben Farrow of Lakota. The engine was a single-cylinder affair typical of those in use at the time. The boiler was the main body and the steam-activating mechanism rested on top of it. This mechanism was not designed for high-speed operation and its low number of revolutions per minute (RPM) dictated the need for a large pulley to maintain the proper RPM on the thresher cylinder. A small coal bin and water storage tank were located adjacent to the operator's platform at the rear, and the smokestack was at the front, where pulsating puffs of exiting steam assisted the removal of combustion gases (draft).

In addition to the controls necessary for the proper operation of the steam-activated mechanism, there was one to engage the gears driving the wheels. Since there was only one gear ratio and no clutch, this mechanism was rather simple. There was no need for a clutch because the engine was never in motion when the gears were engaged.

Because the machine was used primarily as a stationary power plant, its steering mechanism was unsophisticated. The front wheels were attached to an axle that was pivoted for steering by the use of chains wrapped around a horizontal shaft rotated by the steering wheel.

Although smaller than a locomotive, it was still a large machine and its similar appearance and operation made it no less an attention getter. The large quantity of black coal smoke from its stack was a signal to the surrounding countryside that a steamer was present and performing its important task. When this snorting, steaming monster was on the road pulling the threshing machine, everyone stopped to watch.

During a typical day, threshing began in the early forenoon after the dew had disappeared from the grain. Except for a dinner break, the work continued into the evening. The farmers in the ring did all the bundle and grain hauling and one man operated the threshing machine and another operated the water wagon. (More on this on page 103.) Ben Farrow was in charge of the operation and controlled the steam engine.

The proper operation of a steam engine required not only using oil cans and grease cups for the timely lubrication of all bearings, but also a thorough knowledge of boilers. Sufficient coal had to be kept in the fire box to keep the steam pressure up, and the water level *had* to be maintained within a critical range noted on the water gauge. If steam pressure became too high, a safety valve automatically released steam until the pressure was in the acceptable range, but if the water level fell below the top of the fire box or flues, the steel could become red hot and lose its strength, permitting the engine to blow up. Obviously, the owners did not use inexperienced personnel to operate their engines.

The farmer whose grain was being threshed furnished a wagonload of coal, which was conveniently placed near the engine. The water wagon operator maintained the water level in the engine storage tank and the engine operator controlled the injection of water into the boiler.

Because only the escaping steam and the clanking of its clumsy mechanisms contributed noise to the environment, steam engines were much quieter than tractors. The rhythmic pulses from each power stroke gently moved the engine back and forth providing a peaceful, sleep-inducing setting.

Although most steam engines had only one cylinder, they were more powerful than tractors. They could handle the largest threshing machines with two bundle haulers vigorously unloading simultaneously. My bundle-hauling experiences were to take place later when tractors were used and it was easy to plug a machine when bundles were pitched in too fast. Dad told me on several occasions he had seen where bundle haulers tried to plug a machine powered by a steamer and were unable to do so. The reason, at least in part, why this was true lies in the fact that their pistons were subjected to a power stroke every cycle, while the common four-cycle internal combustion engine receives only one every four cycles.

It should be noted that the single-cylinder steam engine had one deficiency not present in those with two or more cylinders. Occasionally, the engine would stop on dead center between power strokes when neither operating valve was open and the throttle had no effect. It was then necessary to physically rotate the pulley a few degrees to partially open one of the operating valves. This was not a problem with engines of two or more cylinders like those used on railway locomotives. Because the cylinders of these machines were attached to the same crankshaft ninety degrees out of phase with each other, at least one operating valve was always partially open.

The rapid demise of the steam engine could be attributed to the fact that the manpower required for its proper operation was greater than the manpower required for a tractor's operation. Distillate fuels derived from crude oil provided a great deal more energy per pound than coal did, and the tractor did not need water for a medium of energy transfer. The steam engine's use of large quantities of water was particularly labor intensive.

When threshing, the water wagon operator obtained water from the farmer's stock tank using a hand pump attached to the wagon. At the engine, the operator used the same pump to place the water in the engine storage tank. When sufficient water was available at the stock tank and threshing was taking place nearby, one person could adequately take care of this operation, although the hand pumping was physically tiring. However, when the stock tank ran dry, which was not an unusual occurrence with the heavy demand placed on it during threshing, the water wagon person had to find another source, generally a nearby neighbor's tank. This long-distance hauling could be time-consuming and delays were not welcomed by the engine operator. When threshing or operating an engine far from water, the water wagon operator's job was not an enviable one.

I know of no case in Iowa where the steam engine was used to pull farm machinery, but they were used in this manner in some states and in Canada. Its most popular use in the field was for plowing, where it could pull a plow that had as many as twelve bottoms. When used for this purpose, logistical support was more of a problem since the engine was moving about distant fields making the delivery of coal and water more time-consuming.

The last romantic chapter of the steam engine was written when tractors of sufficient size and reliability made their appearance. The popularity of steam engines at farm equipment museums is indicative of the esteem in which they are held.

AUXILIARY POWER

As farm equipment became more sophisticated, greater use was made of machines containing rapidly moving parts. The power to activate these parts came from horses and the use of bull wheels. These wheels were geared to the mechanisms, providing them with the proper operating RPMs when the horses were walking at a normal pulling speed. Lugs, or knobs, on the wheels' rims prevented skidding along the ground during forward movement.

When these machines were actively engaged in cutting grain, making bundles, and so on, it was important to maintain forward momentum since slowing down or stopping frequently resulted in a slug plugging the machinery. It was then necessary to use a hand crank that was provided with the machine to free the mechanism.

Picking corn by hand was one of the most unpleasant and time-consuming tasks on the farm (see page 107). The appearance of the mechanical corn picker offered a welcome alternative. Dad purchased one of the first models of these machines, a single-row McCormick Deering, designed to be powered entirely by horses. This machine was one of the most complicated and power-demanding of any on the farm, and since we did not have enough horses for its proper operation, it was Dad's intent to use his tractor to pull it. This provided the setting for experiences typical of farmers gradually changing from horsepower "on the hoof" to tractor power, and the growing pains that resulted.

The corn picker's mechanism included two high speed steel rollers that grasped the entering stalks near the ground and wrung them down between the rollers like clothes being pulled through a washing machine wringer. The protrusions and indentations on these closely fitting rollers pulled the stalks through, but did not permit the ears to follow. The ears were pulled off, swept up and over a set of husking rollers, and dropped into the lower end of the elevator before they were elevated and dropped into a wagon being pulled adjacent to the picker by a team of horses.

Two bull wheels, connected together through a differential, provided the power to activate the mechanism. A small flywheel was attached to a rapidly turning shaft at the rear of the picker where it maintained some degree of momentum when brief power surges were required.

In addition to driving the horses on the picker, the operator had controls to engage the bull wheels, to adjust the height of the fork containing the picking rollers where the stalks entered, and to stop the elevator when going around the end of the field where the wagon operator could not stay adjacent to the picker.

Because momentum had to be maintained when corn stalks were engaged, at least five horses were required to pull this machine. It was known as a "horse killer," and either the horses were given frequent rests or different horses had to be used to keep the machine in operation throughout the day. Some farmers, like my dad, tried to use a tractor in place of horses.

Most tractors in use during the early 1920s were clumsy, inefficient machines designed to be used exclusively for plowing and belt work, and ours was no exception. Dad had used tractors for some time and had recently purchased a used 1919 Hart Parr. It was this tractor he planned to use on the picker. Although primitive by today's standards, this two-cylinder machine proved to be a good one for its intended purpose, which, of course, did not include pulling a picker.

Machinery designed to be pulled by a tractor (plows, etc.) were made to be operated from the tractor, and the newer tractors such as the McCormick Deering had power take-offs where the tractor not only pulled the machine across the field but powered its mechanism directly through the use of rapidly turning shafts without the use of bull wheels. (See page 114.) This was a much more efficient means of power transfer and permitted the machine to be operated for checking purposes while at rest. Our picker permitted the use of such a device, but unfortunately, the Hart Parr was not properly equipped; our tractor would have to pull the picker, powering the mechanism through the bull wheels.

The most effective operation was obviously one where the tractor, picker, and wagon could all be controlled by one man on the tractor, and Dad proceeded to make modifications on this basis.

First, the small two-wheeled carriage at the front of the picker was removed and this portion of the picker was supported on the tractor draw bar. This placed the picker controls closer to the tractor operator, but unfortunately, not close enough to be operated while the tractor was in motion.

Second, a boom was attached to the front of the picker and projected to the right side where the tongue of the wagon was attached. This not only eliminated the need for a wagon operator, but the elevator control could then be set to operate and left in that position because the wagon remained at the picker's side while turning around at the ends of the field.

Upon the completion of these modifications, Dad was ready to use his new picker. He proceeded to the field where he set the picker fork high enough so that the projecting points cleared the hills around the base of the cornstalks while going around the ends of the field, but low enough to pick up most of the stalks that were bent over. The bull wheels were then engaged and picking began.

Difficulties were immediately encountered. For proper operation, the picker fork had to be aligned rather precisely with the incoming row of corn and this was a problem when pulling the picker with our Hart Parr. Not only did it steer like a tractor, where excessive play dictated the need for extensive steering wheel action before the front wheels responded, but the wheel spacing did not lend itself to proper operation between the rows of corn. When cultivating corn the last two times, the cultivator shovels had been set to toss dirt around the base of the cornstalks to kill the weeds and this dirt formed a ridge in drilled corn or hills in checked corn. The wheel spacing on the Hart Parr was such that it could not be driven without the long projecting angle lugs on the rear wheels riding at least partially over these hills, making steering more difficult. The physical exertion required in steering this machine did not permit the operator to use its seat so Dad stood and was soon seen spinning the steering wheel vigorously back and forth while keeping his eye on the fork of the picker.

Dad gave this operation a good try but it quickly became apparent that too much corn was being left in the field; the use of the Hart Parr on this picker was not practical.

Because the tractor could not be used and we did not have enough horses for a complete horse operation, other means for powering the machine were sought. The engine in a 1918 Chevrolet car Dad had junked was still operable. Using the engine to power the mechanism of the picker while it was being pulled across the field with three horses appeared feasible. Dad and Wilbur proceeded to mount this engine on the picker and make all the necessary modifications.

A chain sprocket wheel was attached to the drive shaft that extended from the transmission of the engine, and another one replaced the small flywheel of the picker. Clutch and throttle controls were placed near the operator; the small front carriage was put back in place and the boom arm was removed. Picking would now proceed with Dad operating the picker and Wilbur the wagon.

This arrangement proved possible but was not without its difficulties. The main drive chain going from the engine to the picker mechanism operated at high speeds and Dad had used a low-speed chain from discarded machinery. This low-speed chain had oil holes in each link and these had to be oiled frequently with an oil can. Unfortunately, they wore rapidly and broke without warning, violently casting the chain aside and immediately creating danger for any humans in the chain's flight path.

The picker continued to be used in this fashion until the Chevrolet engine failed. Dad then purchased a used V-2 garden tractor and mounted its engine on the picker. Picking proceeded satisfactorily with the use of this engine until an oil cock in the oil pan was accidentally jarred loose without being noticed, and the loss of oil caused the bearing that attached the two connecting rods to the crankshaft to burn out. Because parts for this engine were no longer available, Dad and Wilbur made their own bearing by melting old babbitt metal and pouring it between the crankshaft and connecting rods while they were held firmly in place. Although it was necessary to repeat the process later, this homemade bearing worked satisfactorily for some time. The picker was used in this fashion until this engine died later at Ledyard and a Model T engine replaced it.

When first introduced, the picker noted above was quite popular. Some farmers used horses exclusively for its operation, but there were many like Dad who used engines in one form or another to reduce the need for horses. Efficient two-row pickers with power take-off, exclusively designed for use with a tractor, soon followed and rapidly replaced this machine. It does not appear to be a common item in agricultural museums.

Recreational Pursuits

AT HOME

During the 1920s the variety of commercially available recreational toys was limited, especially so in rural areas and small towns, and most were obtained from catalogs. Television was unknown and the few radio programs on the air were not youth oriented. Young people were expected to entertain themselves with the limited facilities available, and this they did.

The presence of horses quite naturally provided the opportunity for equestrian activities, but they were not as extensively pursued as might be imagined. Our horses were draft horses whose backs had never known the presence of a saddle and few of them had ever been ridden. When field work was in progress, they were not available for recreational purposes even on Sunday, which was also a day of rest for them. When the opportunity did present itself, Dan, one of the draft horses, was Wilbur's friendly companion.

Riding Dan was the least sophisticated means of using his unique abilities, and it had its limitations. Draft horses seldom trot or gallop and their natural gait is not a spirited one. When riding such an animal, the rider does not become one with the horse and when unseasoned, the constant up-and-down motion of the high backbone presents an open invitation to a degree of soreness best left unexperienced. If performed often enough and long enough, bareback riding would develop a toughness in that portion of the anatomy in contact with the horse, but such was generally not the case with farm boys. It was not an activity engaged in as frequently as it was on western ranches.

Wilbur's occasional ride on Dan was, no doubt, a pleasant diversion from farm work, but I recall no exciting races with other panting clodhoppers, all exerting their muscular bodies into a frenzy to keep their noses somewhat in front of the others. The use of Dan to pull recreational vehicles did not subject a rider to the same degree of battering and this was the way his abilities were generally used.

As previously noted, our buggy was no longer in use as a means of family transportation; it had become one of Wilbur's recreational vehicles. Because its appearance did not differ from others then in use, Wilbur decided to give it a distinctive covered wagon look by using some old discarded grain binder canvases for a top. He used this rig to tour the neighborhood, occasionally taking Dolores and me with him.

In the winter, when snow made use of the buggy undesirable, Wilbur used Dan on the cutter. The seating facilities on this vehicle had been removed or so modified that travel required a degree of devotion possessed by few, but this did not preclude its use by Wilbur and his friends. Its lack of facilities did not lend itself to an invitation for Dolores or me to participate.

Dan had received his final reward before I was old enough to subject him to my whims of fancy. I was to experience some "plow-horse" bareback riding later at Ledyard. Unfortunately, by that time the buggy was in parts and the cutter ceased to exist. Buggies and cutters were rapidly disappearing and horse-drawn recreational vehicles did not play a part in my future.

Very few farms were electrified and the use of single-cylinder gasoline engines was common. We had several; one was a small, air-cooled model that had been purchased to use with a car generator to charge storage batteries. Its performance proved to be less than ideal and Dad soon gave it to Wilbur for recreational use. Using parts from discarded farm machinery, engines, and cars, Wilbur used this engine to power vehicles and machines of his own design. Perhaps it was fortunate that when possession of this engine passed on to me, it was no longer operable. I did not possess the infinite patience required for its proper operation.

The tree-lined dredge ditch bordering the west side of our farm provided the setting for a few simple water-related activities. In the summer Dolores and I occasionally went swimming in the shallow, silt-laden water, wading about in the mud like ancient amphibians seeking a better environment. While we were so engaged, Wilbur reduced the population of a more suitable inhabitant, a catfish generally referred to as a bullhead. He did so by using a simple stick with string, cork, and hook attached and indigenous worms for bait.

Great care was necessary when cleaning these fish. Their heads constituted a substantial portion of their carcasses and the protruding barbels could sting and were best left undisturbed by bare hands. After their careful removal with the entrails, the small, bony remains were delivered to Mother for preparation. The flesh was very tasty, but the effort exerted in bone removal discouraged its consumption. Choking on bones was part of the dining ceremony when this dish was on the menu.

During the fall and winter, Wilbur trapped muskrats, as well as an occasional mink or weasel, along this stream and made a few cents selling their hides. This activity involved setting traps, removing an animal's hide from its body, and placing the hide on a rack to dry. However, because the returns from these hunting excursions were so meager, few people spent much time developing the required techniques.

In the winter when ice in the ditch had developed sufficient thickness, Wilbur used our clamp-on ice skates for recreation. The skates had a nasty habit of working themselves loose from the shoes and coming off at the most inopportune moment. In order to prevent this, a key had to be carried at all times and used frequently to tighten the clamps. Occasionally, a long excursion was made down the stream to adjacent neighborhoods. During such ventures, caution was advised because some farmers had placed barbed wire fences across the stream. An intimate embrace with these fences was not recommended when traveling at high speed.

During the long winter evenings, the kitchen became our playground. Here we often made popcorn or ice cream and fired up Wilbur's steam engine. We raised our own popcorn (Japanese Hulless) and it was never in short supply, nor was the butter, which was generously drizzled on top. Ice cream was made less frequently but was no less welcomed. Our two-quart, hand-operated metal freezer was similar to those currently available. Mother used pure cream in the mix and the result was an ice cream that is yet to be duplicated by any commercially manufactured product.

Wilbur's toy steam engine was much more sophisticated

than those I have recently seen for sale. It closely duplicated the features of the larger engines, including their cylinders, valves, and so on. The boiler water was heated by wicks protruding from a covered tray that contained wood alcohol, and belts were used to power a few simple accessories.

Most of the time our parents were in the living room when these activities were taking place, but there were occasions when Dad joined us in the kitchen to develop pictures. We had a simple box camera, which the children used, and its film was commercially developed, but Dad had a sophisticated camera for taking "good" pictures, and these he developed himself.

His camera was the kind you focused on a frosted glass plate while viewing the scene, which was upside down, from under a hood. The film slide was inserted and the shutter operated by cable. Dad also had a timing device to operate the shutter, permitting him to get in the picture. He developed his film in the kitchen sink at night with a red covering over the glass chimney of a kerosene lamp. Most of the good pictures we now possess of our family were taken and developed by him. (The poor quality snapshots reproduced in this book were not developed by Dad.)

Our first radio was a battery-operated Crosley that required the use of an aerial wire strung from the top of a tall pole at the house to another pole positioned approximately one hundred feet away. It could be heard through the use of a separate speaker or earphones. My access to this instrument was limited and I do not recall it being a great source of entertainment; it was an adult plaything, and most adults showed more interest in receiving remote stations than in the content of messages. My only recollection of its reception was the news of Lindbergh's successful flight over the Atlantic. Radio's popularity soon prompted Dad to purchase a new larger and better one, a Fada. This radio, encased in a wooden box with a black horn-shaped speaker sitting on top, was to be of more interest to me when we lived at Ledyard.

THE PARTY PHONE

Although not considered a recreational facility, our party-line phone was not without an element of entertainment. Each party on our line had a code consisting of short and long rings, and when any party was called, all phones responded. To call someone on your line, you held the receiver down with your left hand and turned the small generator crank vigorously with your right, generating the current necessary to ring all the bells on the line. This was done in short and long spurts in the desired code. To call long distance or other party lines, it was necessary to go through the operator in town.

The degree of curiosity possessed by normal humans compelled many to listen to conversations not intended for their ears. This was called "rubbering"; it reduced signal strength, and hearing became difficult. Rubbering forced speakers to shout to be heard, and sarcastic references to uninvited listeners were common.

No quicker means of news dispersal has ever been devised than a phone call on a party line. It seems that all parties had a member conveniently positioned for a quick response, and the lines were soon humming with activity when juicy bits of gossip became available.

After we left the Lakota farm, we did without phone service. (If I recall correctly, the service charge for a phone was fifty cents per month.) The folks were not to have such service again until 1945, when phones were different and party lines were limited and had fewer members.

VISITING

Although we lived quite some distance from our parents' hometown, a number of relatives lived nearby and their close proximity provided a setting for frequent informal visits. Dad had a sister who lived with her family on a farm three miles southeast of us, a cousin who lived with her family on a farm eight miles northwest of us near Elmore, Minnesota, and Mother had a niece who was married to the brother of Mrs. Roelfsema, a nearby neighbor. Other relatives of various closeness lived near Buffalo Center and Ledyard. Visits were not limited to relatives, of course, and we frequently got together with the John Winterses, our neighbors across the road.

My participation in these social affairs is fondly remembered, but those to the Roelfsema farm have a special poignancy. Their son Ivan had a Shetland pony and it added a new dimension to our visits. Horses respect good riders and a mutual admiration had developed between Ivan and his pony, but such was not the case with me. I admired Ivan's riding skills and wanted to duplicate them, but my clumsy, amateur performances quickly convinced the pony that I was a dude he could control with ease, and he proceeded to do so.

The removal of a rider from its back is, for a horse, the ultimate show of disdain, and this was precisely the course of action the pony followed. His favorite trick was to let me develop some degree of confidence in my riding ability, wait until at least one person was available to record the performance, quickly pass before the viewer, and stop suddenly, throwing me over his head and onto the ground. I would then pick myself up and attempt a lighthearted comment to the visibly amused audience, perhaps implying that it was all part of the scenario.

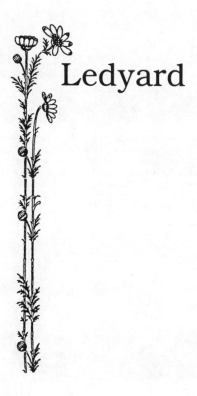

Ledyard

Ledyard house, garage, and chicken house, 1929. The chicken house is on the left, and the garage in the center. The large pans leaning against the garage were used by the former tenant to make sorghum. The shanty stands in front of the kitchen of the house.

Ledyard barn, 1929.

Ledyard Consolidated School, 1929.

Ledyard school band, circa 1935.

Kenneth, Dolores, Anna Marie, Mother, and the Model T Roadster, 1929. Our overflow oats bin is on the left and our shanty on the right.

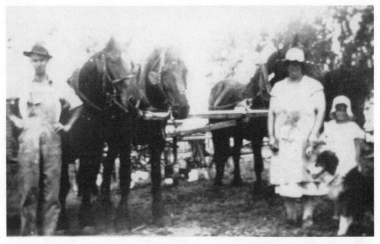

Wilbur, Mother, Anna Marie, and Shep by the two-row cultivator, 1935.

Threshing, 1930.

Shelling corn, 1934. The sheller, shown partially on the right, was an early model mounted on its own chassis and powered by a belt.

Bringing in a newborn calf, 1934. Kenneth is on the stoneboat and Anna Marie is standing in the background. Note the box for cream cans on the Whippet.

New Farm, New Challenge

Although I was not aware of it at the time, events were taking place that would bring our life on the Lakota farm to a close. Grandfather died in 1927, and the next year the folks decided to buy their own farm.

After driving by to inspect farms for sale in the vicinity, it became apparent that the funds they had available limited their choice to one of two farms; both were 160 acres in size and in need of improvements. A farm located two and one-half miles southwest of Ledyard was their choice. They purchased it from the superintendent of banking of the state of Iowa as receiver of the County Savings Bank of Algona, Iowa, on November 24, 1928, for the total sum of $13,200. Six hundred dollars was paid at the time of purchase and $600 on March 1, 1929, and a first mortgage for $12,000 from the Traveler's Insurance Company was assumed. Plans then proceeded for our move to this farm.

MOVING TO LEDYARD

Conventional moving day for Iowa farmers was March 1, and although it was our intent to move on that day, dirt roads frequently assured the fallibility of the "plans of mice and men," which proved to be the case with us. When moving short distances, cattle were driven along the road and household and other miscellaneous items were transported by horse-drawn vehicles, but the distance had to be short enough so that assisting

47

neighbors could return home the same day. The shortest distance to our Ledyard farm was seven miles due west and one mile south, a sufficient amount to dictate the need for haste. Unfortunately, five miles of this route was over a road that was seldom used. Because it was generally impassable in the winter, there was some doubt whether it would become so in time for our move. The only other feasible route was south on Highway 169 for two miles, west five miles on Highway 9, and then a mile north to the farm, nearly ten miles each way. This route was really too long to expect neighbors to assist us and Dad felt it prudent to delay our move one day.

On the first, the farmer moving onto our Lakota farm found the road from the east passable and he proceeded with his move. This complicated matters. The presence of two families in the same house, with two different owners having animals in the same grossly overcrowded, appurtenant facilities, made it imperative that we make our move regardless of the consequences. Dad made the necessary plans to move on the second, using both routes. The plan was for Wilbur and John Winters, Jr., to ride horseback and drive our cattle over the long route, while all horse-drawn vehicles would take the short route. Phone calls for assistance were made.

Early on the morning of the second, neighbors appeared with hayracks, wagons, and teams. When all the vehicles were loaded, they formed a caravan and proceeded slowly down the road. The five miles of questionable road began a mile west at Telkamp's corner. The first vehicle had to break a trail for those behind. I was too young to experience the trials and tribulations they were to encounter, but sufficient horse and manpower was present to keep the caravan moving.

On arrival at the Ledyard farm, it was discovered that the farmer moving from this farm had left some of his furnishings in the house. Because our move had taken considerable time and those assisting us could not delay their return home, our furniture was moved in and placed at any available spot. Mother could do little to clean up until the other farmer had removed all of his belongings, and she could not make the place livable before some of our important furnishings such as stoves and beds were assembled and correctly placed. This house had one less bedroom than our previous house and no front room, so some furnishings had to be discarded and others squeezed into space available in a small adjacent building we called the shanty. Because the house was small, we had plenty of confusion.

While Mother's task was a very difficult one, Dad and Wilbur had their own problems to solve. After setting up the stoves and beds, they had to go out and attend our newly arrived animals, placing them in new and insufficient protective shelters.

Those who have moved their own household furnishings are aware of the difficulties involved in moving from one residence to another, but this task is considerably more complicated when more than one household is involved, all parties are moving the same day, and one of them encounters a delay. When the task includes several kinds of animals and their feed, it is obvious that a great deal of coordination, infinite patience, and a tremendous amount of work are required for successful completion. With neighborly assistance, we managed to move enough of our possessions that day so that we could move the rest by ourselves. This took time, several months in fact. However, we were established in our new environment, where our lives would differ substantially from that which we had experienced before.

SETTLING IN

There is a certain air about new environments that quickly permeates the mind; some have a pleasant aura, others a more somber and sobering cast. The latter was more apparent as we settled into our new home. Any move made from a place where happy memories abide is accompanied by apprehension, but when such a move is made to a lonely setting where physical conditions reflect past economic distress, it cannot be said that euphoria follows.

Although I was only seven years old, the move to new surroundings disturbed me, and Mother's concern about lack of cleanliness in the house added to my depression.

The physical condition of the farm's improvements were indicative of those where the American dream had not proven to be within grasp; it had become a rental and was what real estate sales personnel refer to as "a fixer-upper." Extensive repair was required and a tremendous amount of hard work lay ahead for all the adults. However, my parents no doubt faced the future with the enthusiasm that comes with an opportunity to improve one's self.

The House and Related Structures

The house consisted of a kitchen, living room, and bedroom on the first floor, and two bedrooms upstairs. The kitchen had been a part of and detached from a former house; its open gable end had been placed against the siding of a newer story-and-a-half portion, forming a less than perfect union. We were to experience some difficulty in eliminating drafts and there were occasions in the winter when small amounts of snow could be found on the kitchen floor. With essentially the same furnishings we had had in our former kitchen, this smaller area was somewhat cramped.

There was no cistern, sink, or hand pump as there had been at Lakota. Our wash water had to be discarded into a five-gallon pail. This pail and the "slop pail" used to store edible garbage for the hogs were kept in an inconspicuous place. The one-bushel cob basket and old wood-holding boiler were kept near the range. Stick matches were kept in a metal container that hung on the wall by the stove and a kerosene can was placed on the floor nearby. A mirror was conveniently located on the wall behind the washstand.

The furnishings in the living room were judiciously located so that when the hatchway in the floor that led to the small cellar needed to be opened, extensive furniture rearranging was not required. Entry into the folks' bedroom on the first floor was through a draped, double door opening from the living room.

The steep stairway from the living room entered the north bedroom upstairs and entry to the south bedroom was through this room. All beds were placed against the side walls where the gable of the one-and-a-half-story structure reduced the ceiling height. There was a small closet in the south bedroom and an alcove between the two rooms used for storage. During the winter the stovepipe from the heating stove in the living room below passed through an air clearance fixture on the second floor and entered a brick chimney in the roof above. This exposed stovepipe eliminated some of its heat in the south bedroom. (This pipe was dismantled and stored with the stove during the summer.)

Kerosene lamps were used to light the house except for the living room where our reading took place. There a ceiling mantle fixture was installed as part of a gasoline lighting system that utilized white gasoline, pressurized in an acetylene-type tank by a car tire pump. Wire-sized tubing was used to feed the gasoline to the mantles. Care was necessary when lighting these mantles since flames would frequently burst forth. Gas leakage could also be a problem if the system was not properly installed or maintained. Gasoline camping-type lanterns were in use in some homes, and we later used a chrome-plated model with a detachable pump in lieu of the installed system. Later still, an Aladdin kerosene lamp, using a round wick to feed a flame to the mantle's ash, was used. Its fuel was less dangerous and did not have to be pressurized.

The shanty was a small, separate building next to the kitchen. It contained a cooking range, laundry facilities, and storage for items we could not keep in the house. At Lakota, a gasoline engine with a belt running through an opening in the wall had been used to power the washing machine, but shortly after our move to Ledyard, Mother got a new Dexter washing machine with its own Briggs and Stratton engine.

The one structure most often referred to when discussing life without indoor plumbing was one with many names—outhouse, backhouse, privy, toilet, and others best left unprinted. For obvious reasons, they were never referred to as restrooms or bathrooms. Regardless of title, they were always located in back of the house where they could not be seen by entering guests, and far enough away so that unusual acoustical disturbances could not be heard or intense odoriferous gases detected by sensitive humans in the house.

Invariably, they were two-holers, although the need for the second hole is unknown since the interior environment was not conducive to fellowship. Ventilation and adequate lighting were provided in our facility by the spaces between the siding boards, which had shrunk apart. These spaces also provided a convenient means of entry for undesirable inhabitants—flies—which not only reproduced in fantastic numbers, but also forced the quick departure of all occupants. Our structure had no decorative feature, but some had a small crescent placed in or above the entrance. A few comments regarding activities associated with this structure are in order.

Victorian attitudes did not permit use of more descriptive words, so the elimination of human waste was delicately referred to as "number one" or "number two," with number two requiring a paper document for a proper completion. Much has been said about the use of catalogs for this purpose, which is all true, including the lack of a desirable roughness on the part of the slick pages.

No doubt lines have formed to use the bathroom in one-bathroom houses serving six people, but extensive traffic to our outside facility was never in evidence. To get there, we had to go out the kitchen door, around the shanty, and head due north, and such a journey was not made until nature's call became quite urgent and lower bowel activity dictated the need for speed. Caution was advised when approaching a sprinter who had used laxatives. An imaginary element of danger was not unknown when these journeys were made on a dark night without the use of a flashlight, and under these circumstances, I have reason to believe a few speed records were broken.

Bladders operated on a shorter time frame and our rural environment provided the setting for unique ways of disposing of liquid wastes. Before going to bed, darkness permitted me to find relief in an area outside the house, and the distance of this area from the house was dictated by the weather; the more inclement the weather, the closer this area was to the door. Standing in the doorway and aiming at a nearby snowbank was an act not entirely unknown to me in subzero weather.

I recall no great enthusiasm for getting out of a warm bed in our unheated house at 3:00 A.M. to take a casual stroll through the snow to relieve myself. A bedpan in the form of a one-gallon syrup can was occasionally used. The drum roll response of liquid hitting its bottom usually brought other occupants of the room to attention.

Obviously, our outside facility was provided not only for our use, but for the convenience and comfort of our guests. However, it soon became apparent that all of them had unusually good bladder control—I do not recall any of them using this facility after an initial introduction.

Although our facility was conveniently located for those in or near the house, it was much less so for those occupied elsewhere. When nature called while working in the southwest forty, I did not make a mad, half-mile dash to use the outhouse. Because our farm equipment did not have paper dispensers, it was necessary to use any flora available, and everything but thistle leaves was used. There were times when even this material was in short supply and then advance preparations were a necessity.

When around the barnyard, the use of cobs was not un-

New Farm, New Challenge

known. However, they were not popular for anyone with hemorrhoids, and even those of us free from hemorrhoids found it important to choose the correct specimens. The best were newly shelled with a velvet touch, and the worst were those the pigs had slobbered over and left to dry in barnyard refuse. When good specimens were found, they were kept in my overall pockets to be used later, such as the times in the southwest forty perhaps.

Outhouses required little maintenance except for an occasional move. The anaerobic organisms that digest solids in septic tanks did not find the availability of air in the pits to their liking; consequently, the solids did not liquify and seep away. When the accumulation had reached an elevation where it threatened to pucker up against the lower extremities of the occupants, it was time to move the structure. A new location was then chosen nearby and a pit with the proper dimensions was dug. The horizontal dimensions of this pit were carefully selected; the pit had to be as large as possible, and still be able to support the structure and any occupants.

After the pit had been dug, the outhouse was moved to the new location. This was done carefully since it had to be moved by hand and those of us involved had no desire to step into (or on top of) the old pit. The age-old problem encountered by Halloween pranksters of stepping forward just as the structure overturned and thus ending up deeply embedded in night soil was one we made an effort to avoid.

Although somewhat of a paradox, the introduction of flush toilets in rural houses did not always meet with universal acclaim. The use of a separate facility located some distance from the house was so ingrained that there were those who were reluctant to use an inside facility when others were present. I recall being at an aunt's house shortly after they had installed a flush toilet and she told Mother she did not use the inside facility when company was present. No explanation was necessary.

OTHER FARM BUILDINGS

Some of our other structures were of eye-catching quality. It is possible that all had come in contact with paint briefly at their birth, but evidence of it was now lacking and their condition had deteriorated to the point where cosmetic applica-

53

tions were superfluous. Respect for old age demands a quick look.

The barn was a simple gable structure with horse stalls along each side, a hay storage area in the center, and a lean-to along the back. The lean-to was the cow barn. The stalls along the north side of the barn were used as calf pens and farrowing pens for sows. There was no place for the separator or miscellaneous storage, so a room was quickly constructed for this purpose in the hay storage area at the front of the barn.

Since there was no haymow, hay was stacked in the central storage area up into the gable area. The barn had the usual large haymow door and there was a hay carrier track attached to the peak of the gable, but there was no carrier, rope, or means of lifting hay. (Slings had been used at Lakota and a fork was used later at Manly.)

The barn's condition was such that maintenance had to be restricted to that necessary to provide a sufficient degree of protection to give the animals a fighting chance for survival during severe winter weather. If body heat was to raise the subzero temperatures a few degrees, it was necessary to plug up cracks in the roof and walls. The shingles had weathered to the point where their resistance to rain was not as stubborn as it should have been. Weather damage was compounded by interior artillery practice. The use of BB guns was no problem and the damage from 22-caliber rifles was generally acceptable when used judiciously (I must confess to some of these activities myself), but previous occupants had apparently used 12-gauge shotguns and they displayed a distinct dislike for the integrity of the barn's roof.

Although the location of doors in exterior walls was evident, the condition of these walls was such that they encouraged maverick animals to occasionally make their own means of egress. I recall one instance when a cow decided to make a door out of a window and, unfortunately, succeeded. Since two doors were an unnecessary luxury, a few boards, some nails, and a hammer were needed to restore the quaint architecture of the building.

The chicken house was also a simple gabled structure with a lean-to in back. In the main portion, two-by-two wood roosts were placed approximately eighteen inches apart and twelve inches above the ground on posts. Hens laid their eggs in wooden boxes located around the interior perimeter. Except in winter, the door was always open and the chickens were free to roam about the farmyard.

On the Lakota farm a kerosene heated incubator located in the cellar under the house had been used to hatch chicks, but it had been discarded during our move. During the first few years at Ledyard, the lean-to in back was used in the spring by Mother as a brooder house for setting hens, and at other times as additional space for laying hens. Later, as noted on page 132, a small separate brooder house was built and used for this purpose.

Although evidence of the use of firearms was not apparent in the chicken house, roof leakage was not unknown during heavy rains. Occasionally, a chicken could be seen sitting on a roost directly under a leak, refusing to move over a few inches to escape it.

Our oats bin was a simple 6′ × 12′ rectangular structure with a roof sloping towards the back. There were removable panels on the upper portion of the front to permit the scooping of oats from a wagon into the bin. It was in good condition but did not have the capacity to hold all of our crop, and another building, similar to our shanty, was used for additional storage.

The garage was a rectangular, flat-roofed structure large enough for one car and a tool shed in front. I recall no instance where its architecture was commented upon with favor.

There was no hog house, and since the barn was not large enough to hold all of our hogs, a building was erected for their use. It consisted of poles embedded in the ground, roof joists and 1″ × 12″ boards for the siding and roof. The upper portion of the east end was left unsheathed to permit the entry of light, and removable panels were used as dutch doors.

Because the hog house was open to the elements on one end, the hogs had to keep warm in the winter by burying themselves in large amounts of straw. Sometimes during the winter, when we entered the building, we could see snow on top of the straw, and the presence of hogs was not apparent until we stepped on one. Hogs approaching maturity did not appear to be adversely affected by this environment, but the goal of getting hogs to weigh two hundred pounds in six months was obviously not attained under such conditions.

There was no corncrib, so one was constructed by using poles embedded in the ground, yet tall enough for three tiers of snow fence. The floor consisted of boards placed over logs, and when the crib was full, corn bundles were placed on the sloping pile of corn to facilitate drainage. The rectangular structure was placed adjacent to the hog yard for ease in feeding the hogs.

OTHER FEATURES

There was a small orchard southeast of our house, and although it had a number of old apple trees, they were not very productive. We had a hand-operated spray pump that was placed in a barrel and moved about the orchard by a team and wagon. We had used it extensively at Lakota, but I do not recall spraying at Ledyard. A new orchard was started south of the Ledyard house but when we lost the farm, it was abandoned and never became productive. The grafting activities Dad had pursued at Lakota were no longer in evidence.

Our land appeared to be flat, but there were low spots where the lack of drainage permitted the forming of ponds in the spring. These ponds did not disappear until it was too late to plant crops. The permanent pasture was shaped so that it encompassed the larger ponds and cultivation was restricted to the better drained higher ground. There were several acres in the southwest corner of the farm that were unbroken, original prairie. Dad began tiling the farm during the summer of 1929 by connecting to an intake in the Ed Donji farm to our south. This tiling was accomplished by using a trenching spade with an open back in wet clay and a solid one in granular material. A tiling tool was used to form a round bed for the tile, and flowing water was used to ensure a positive drainage gradient.

The fences were in poor condition and the only hog tight, woven wire ones were on the property lines and around our hog yard. As a result, we could never let our hogs out into the fields. Exits for cattle from barnyards containing both hogs and cattle used a wood barrier high enough for the cattle to jump over but not the hogs.

Highway 9, which ran east-west from Swea City past Gerled (no longer noted on Iowa maps) to Lakota, was a gravel road that would be paved later. Access to this road from our farm was over one mile of an unimproved dirt road. This road made sure that the experiences previously noted would not be forgotten by those of us too young to fully appreciate them.

WHICH HOMETOWN?

Everyone needs a hometown, a community to call your own, but how does one give allegiance to several at the same time? Ledyard, two and one-half miles to our northeast, was where we went to school, but we continued to shop and go to church in Lakota six miles to our southeast. When giving our address, we had to note an RFD (rural free delivery) route out of Bancroft, Iowa, eight miles to the southwest, and to further confuse this picture, when telling people how to get to our farm, we always said "one mile north of Gerled."

Perhaps divided loyalties contributed to my feeling of isolation, but lack of close neighbors my age intensified the feeling. The William Schodendorf family owned a two hundred-acre farm in the southwest corner of our section and we visited with them regularly since Mrs. Schodendorf was a sister of my uncle Riender Johnson, but they had no children my age. Regular contact with my peers was now limited to school and church, two entirely different groups. I was rather shy and did not find these conditions suitable for the development of a sense of bravado or superiority deemed by some to be so necessary for successful interaction with others.

Ledyard Consolidated School

Providing instruction for first through twelfth grade, the Ledyard Consolidated School was a modern, brick structure that contained more facilities than small, single school districts could provide on their own. Constructed around 1925 it had indoor plumbing, steam heat, a gymnasium, and sufficient classrooms so that no more than two grades were assigned to each. It did not have a book store, but used books could be obtained on credit, and if not damaged when returned at the end of the year, only a few cents were charged for their use.

The student body was predominantly rural and used the bus transportation that was provided for their convenience. A few outlying districts continued to operate local one-room schools and sent only their high school students to Ledyard.

TRANSPORTATION

Bus routes were established at the beginning of each year so that walking was kept to a minimum; however, our move took place in March and our farm was not serviced by a bus route. Those in charge agreed that the simplest solution would be to reimburse my parents for transporting us to school until the new routes were established in the fall, and we proceeded on that basis. A used Model T Ford Roadster was purchased and Wilbur drove the three of us to school until the end of the school year. That fall bus service was provided to our farm.

The buses we used were not the commercially manufactured kind in use today, but homemade vehicles that displayed the genius of self-expression. Bus owners made their own buses by placing a wood box on a truck chassis, and following their own specifications; the only requirements were that each bus had to have four wheels, be self-propelled, and students had to be able to get inside and survive a ride of several miles over unimproved county roads.

School ended at 4:00 P.M. and at that time, all buses were assembled at the north entrance, each proudly displaying its "box on wheels" construction. The assortment of buses was a study in contrasts; some appeared long, narrow, and unusually high, while others were short, fat, and squatty. Close inspection of their carpentry suggested fabrication techniques of dubious origin.

Entry was generally made up a few steps in the rear, and riders walked in a stooped position to any available space on a plank bench along each side. A few small windows were provided along the sides and the rear window of the truck cab provided an opening for the operator to observe the entry and discharge of students. Although most of them had windows, I do recall one that had windowless openings on the side that were covered with a canvas that could be raised or lowered.

Travel on rural roads was uncomfortable in any vehicle, but especially when sitting on hard benches in a vehicle whose springs were made to resist a heavy load of cattle. When the roads were dry and smooth, they were dusty; when wet, mud dictated the use of chains; and during the winter, snow was often a problem. County snowplows had their priorities—highways were number one and school and mail routes number two, and when the bus routes were not plowed after a heavy snowfall, chains were required and delays were not uncommon.

Although our buses were not attractive and lacked the safety features now present in commercially manufactured vehicles, they served their purpose and I know of no injuries resulting from their use.

ACADEMIC PURSUITS

I was in the third grade when I entered the Ledyard school. Whether due to different textbooks or greater progress therein, all subjects seemed more advanced to me. Although our superintendent tried to instill a never-give-up determination in his students (he called it stick-to-it-iveness) my quest for knowledge left too much to be desired, and this grade was the first of two grades I repeated at this school (the other one was the seventh grade). Once a reputation for being dumb has been established, it is difficult to shake. I quickly developed an intense dislike for school. Suffice it to say I managed to enter high school in the fall of 1936.

EXTRACURRICULAR ACTIVITIES

The learning process is not restricted to academics and during recesses and the noon hour, I was introduced to activities more to my liking.

The playground equipment such as swings and slides was obviously of interest in the lower grades, but the marble game proved to be more of an interest to the older students. It contained an element new to me—playing for keeps. Different degrees of affluence were in evidence here: "commies" (clay marbles) occupied the lower stratum, "steelies" (ball bearings) possessed a slightly higher one, and "glassies" (glass marbles) held the upper echelon. Those who assumed the mantle of leadership were the ones with extensive holdings in a variety of glassies. The availability of bearings from the junk in our grove assisted me in obtaining a toehold in the middle class, but my abilities and resources did not permit elevation to a position of leadership.

Dad did not encourage participation in sports; consequently, I did not play on a regular school team. Practice time for these activities interfered with my work at home. (I was to see only one formal sporting event at this school—a basketball game.) I did, however, join the other boys in playing baseball, basketball, and football in student-assembled teams during our free time.

My left-handedness at bat and right-handedness when throwing a ball added nothing to my baseball playing ability. Unfortunately, my participation in baseball left much to be desired. Basketball, on the other hand, was of more interest to me. Basketball playing was permitted in the gym during the winter, providing the correct shoes were worn. My parents' budget permitted the purchase of one sixty-nine cent pair of tennis shoes for me, but they had to last the entire season. I used the shoes so much that body and sole began to separate before the season was over and repairs were necessary. Because our shoe repair equipment was designed for leather shoes, the canvas and rubber of my tennis shoes had to be repaired by other means. It was necessary for me to cut large rubber bands from an old inner tube to maintain an intimate embrace between the canvas and rubber of my shoes. These bands performed their intended purpose in a less than perfect manner, and their failure invariably took place when I was dribbling madly down the floor while playing to the galleries. (Spectators watched from a passageway above.)

The school did not have a football team. However, whenever a student brought a football to school, we played the game under rules of uncertain origin. Our rules were made as the necessity arose, and they were always interpreted by the ball owner. I recall one year when a student was alone in the possession of a football at the beginning of the season and the success of his team was phenomenal; in fact, it wasn't until another student brought a ball to school that his team ever lost. I do not recall any flying tackles or Statue of Liberty plays. In fact, I don't recall any plays at all. However, I do remember that the rules of sportsmanship and property ownership were firmly established in our receptive minds.

Although he did not encourage participation in sports, Dad liked music and assisted us in its pursuit. Piano lessons were mandatory, and playing a band instrument was looked upon with favor. Dad had played the cornet as a youth in his hometown band, at college, and in the Lakota band. Wilbur had followed in his footsteps using his Holton cornet. I attempted to do the same with a used, fifteen dollar Conn cornet, but as noted later, my pursuit of this activity left much to be desired.

I heard my first debate at this school. Two adults from Ledyard debated the subject "Which is more valuable, the hole in a doughnut or nothing at all?" The lack of apparent substance in this subject intrigued me, and the debate proved to be quite good. The "hole in the doughnut" side maintained that the oxygen in the air of the hole was necessary to sustain life and was, therefore, of inestimable value, while the "nothing at all" side argued that the nitrogen in this air was the source of wartime explosives and the world would be a better place without it. Contacts with politicians since have convinced me that lofty discussions of this nature are a prerequisite for holding public office.

Tending Farm and Home

One of the facts of life concerning the labor intensive family farm of the 1920s was the necessity for all members of the family to perform repetitive tasks, many of a daily nature. Children accepted this as the natural order of things, and progressed from the simple to the more difficult tasks as they matured. Those noted in the following paragraphs are ones Wilbur and I performed at one time or another, and although the list is not complete, it is indicative of their extent.

JUVENILE TASKS

My first chores were obviously of a juvenile nature and mostly consisted of work that assisted Mother in her tasks in and about the house. The acquisition of fuel for our stoves and water for the house and the removal of garbage were prominent among them. In the summer, little wood was used except in the range for heating laundry and bathwater, but in the winter, large quantities of wood were burned in both the range and heating stove. Our buzz saw was located in back of the house and it was there that the logs were hauled, sawed into the proper length of rounds, and split into the proper size to go into the range and heating stove. This became my job as soon as I could swing an axe effectively.

Keeping drinking and wash water in the bucket at the wash

stand was not difficult, but getting water for laundry and for baths was. I began with medium-size buckets but soon progressed to two five-gallon used paint cans. This water had to be pumped by hand at the well and carried approximately two hundred feet to the house.

When getting small amounts of water from the well, such as that used at the house, we pumped it by hand, but when filling our round-ended steel stock tank, a horizontal Fairbanks Morse engine was used to power a pump jack. This gasoline engine was typical of the many then in use on farms. Before starting, the grease cups on its exposed crankshaft and connecting rod were given a turn, the oil dripper, which lubricated the cylinder, was turned on, and a six-volt Hot Shot battery (or four one and one-half-volt round dry cell batteries in a series) was connected to a coil and the engine breaker to provide the spark. The engine was cranked by hand. Its intake valve was activated by the vacuum created during the intake cycle and the governor controlled its speed by depressing the exhaust valve.

When cranking this engine and at other times when the engine was running and we wanted the pump jack disengaged, the flat belt, which was used to transfer power from the engine to the pump jack, was placed over an idling pulley on the pump jack. After the engine was started, the belt was pushed by pressing a stick against its side and moving it onto an adjacent pulley, activating the pumping mechanism.

It was necessary to fill the stock tank at least once every day, and during the winter the ice covering the tank had to be broken with an axe before pumping could begin. Occasionally, it was too cold to get the engine started and then all pumping was done by hand.

Horses and cattle drank water from the stock tank adjacent to the well, but the calves and hogs had no access to this tank, so water had to be hauled to them. Although care had to be exercised, we used an open barrel placed on a stone boat for watering these livestock. The stone boat was a small raft consisting of planks nailed on two 4″ × 4″ wood runners shaped to slide over the ground. It was pulled by a horse and apparently got its name from hauling large rocks from the field to a disposal area. Water easily splashed out of this container; unfortunately, starting with a full barrel and ending with a bucket full was not an uncommon occurrence. I preferred using two five-gallon pails and carrying the water by hand. Delivering water in this fashion made me appreciate the amount consumed, and during hot weather, this was great indeed. Every time I saw one of the animals eliminate liquids, an involuntary flexing of my arm muscles took place, and I believe the animals sensed this because whenever I approached a group of them, a well-orchestrated display of hydraulics took place, a display that could rival the fountains of Tivoli.

MILKING

During the summer, the cows had to be brought in from the pasture to be milked morning and evening, and our dog, Shep, was always my faithful companion on these forays. He was not trained to get the animals by himself, but he always assisted me.

Each cow was assigned a stanchion in the barn. Metal stanchions could be purchased, but like most farmers', ours were homemade, consisting of two vertical 2" × 4"s placed wide enough apart to allow space for a cow's neck when closed. One of the uprights was rigidly fixed in the supporting frame and the other was hinged at the bottom so that a cow's head could pass between them when open. After their heads were through the stanchions, the hinged upright would be closed and a block dropped into place to keep it there.

We milked an average of twelve cows and it was a chore that had to be done on time. I joined the privileged group that included Mother and Dolores at quite an early age, starting with an old cow who no doubt had experienced every kind of udder manipulation known to man.

Milking was done from the right side of the cow, while sitting on a stool consisting of an eight-inch long piece of 4" × 4" timber with a small board nailed to one end. The milk bucket was held between our legs with the left leg immediately in front of the cow's right rear leg.

There were two methods of extracting milk from the milk-producing appendages—wet and dry. The wet approach was called stripping and required the milker to press forefinger and thumb together at the top of the teat and move them down, forcing the milk into the bucket. To prevent friction from stretching this appendage to an intolerable length, lubrication was required, and milk was the only feasible substance available. Therefore, milking by this method was done with wet hands, using the first milk extracted as a lubricant. This slippery activity was not to my liking and I employed the more commonly used dry teat method.

This method began by pressing the forefinger and thumb together at the top of the teat, but instead of forcing the milk out by then pulling them down, the other fingers were progressively tightened around the teat from the top down, forcing the milk out in this manner. A slight downward pull accompanied this action, but a lubricant was not required.

When a heifer became fresh after having a calf, she had to be trained to go into the cow barn and place her head in a stanchion, which was not a simple task in most cases. Her mammary projections were manipulated for the first time by the hand of man in a manner not natural to her. This procedure generally resulted in retaliation by the only means she had available—kicking with her rear legs.

All of us were subjected to kicking occasionally and the defense against a cow attempting a simple kick with her right rear leg is not difficult because the cow has to move her leg forward first and the milker's left leg prevents this. However, when being milked the first time, heifers had a habit of using unorthodox methods of kicking and Dad was the expert in controlling such activity. The result was often an unusual display of man against beast, with extensive bellowing on the part of the heifer and a vocal rendition by Dad.

We had kickers that consisted of U-shaped clamps that were placed over the cows' tendons at the rear of their legs just above the knee and attached together with a chain that was placed firmly around and in front of the legs. This effectively chained a cow's rear legs together, preventing her from raising or kicking with one leg. However, this did not prevent her from jumping up with the rear portion of her body and kicking with both legs. This action was generally straight back and did not endanger Dad, but the successful completion of this maneuver required a degree of physical dexterity and expertise not normally possessed by heifers and they often fell down after attempting it. Dad did little sitting while this was going on and he had to step rapidly backward when the cow fell. It was necessary to remove the kickers so the heifer could get up, only to repeat the process. Eventually, she would tire of the game and permit those physical manipulations that the older cows had learned to accept years before.

Cows that had been milked before and became fresh again, gave little trouble, but Dad always milked them the first few times until they were well established in the old routine. The trauma of losing their calf made them nervous, and the liquid they produced the first few days had to be fed to the calf.

Milking was often performed under less than ideal conditions. That portion of a cow's anatomy used in the milking process hangs rather low and close to the ground, and during certain times of the year, when it was necessary for them to wade through mud and manure, it would be coated with material best left out of the milk bucket. This was frequently the case during the spring thaw when the frost was going out of the ground and the manure pile at the entrance to the cow barn contributed additional moisture to the deep, muddy pathway the cows had to take to get into the barn. At such times, "mudder had to drag her udder through the gutter" and it was then necessary to wash those parts before milking began. Because there was no running water or washing facilities in our barn, we had to wash the udder by hand, using a pail of water. This was not always done in a professional manner and all the material was not always removed. Undesirable material in the bucket was not an unknown.

There were times when uninvited guests insisted in joining us in our milking tasks. The generous amounts of several different kinds of manure found around the farm was, in effect, an elaborate buffet for flies during the summer, and they took full advantage of it to breed in countless numbers. Houseflies were joined by their bloodsucking relatives who used the blood of farm animals, including the cows, for their source of food.

When not in the barn, cows had some defense against these insect attacks by using their tails and occasionally throwing their heads around against their back. However, when in the barn, they could not use their heads, and the milker usually held the cow's tail by placing the end of it between the left knee and the bucket. Cows not being milked could still use their tails. Although the kickers had an attachment to hold the tail, we seldom used them. To reduce the amount of blood that flies could extract from the cows under such conditions, we sprayed with a hand sprayer. This spray was not confined to the cows; it permeated the air, making it rather unpleasant not only for the flies, but also for the milkers. It had a tendency to burn our eyes when mixed with the sweat on our face and arms, and breathing it was not pleasant either.

It soon became evident that our cows did not appreciate losing the use of their tail when being milked, and their means of retaliation was to use this appendage aggressively against the milker performing his or her duties on an adjacent cow. The tail of the cow at a milker's back could not be stilled and its pursuit of fly removal encompassed the milker's face. This was not done in a soft, caressing manner, and there were occasions when unwanted material was deposited in the process.

When cattle were first put on grass, they frequently developed what is sometimes called loose bowels, and loose they were. On such occasions, the viscosity of the extruded material approached that of water and tremendous hydraulic pressure was used with an unbelievably high exit velocity. When expelling this material, the tail was raised to prevent interference with its trajectory, but frequently the bushy end found itself in the field of fire, and then it absorbed an unbelievable amount of this material. The cows then made sure the absorbed quantity was not reduced until milking time in the barn.

When milking under these conditions, the milker could manage the bushy end of the tail of the cow being milked. Unfortunately, placing the tail between his knee and the milk bucket meant the overalls absorbed much of the fluid. However, this did nothing to eliminate tail activity of the cow standing immediately behind the milker. The spacing of milk cows in the barn had been precisely determined so that the bushy end of the cow's tail at the milker's rear would strike the milker directly across the face when swung in a vigorous manner, and when she wound this tail up with many pounds of saturated material on the end, she delivered a devastating blow. The undesirable contents were deposited over the milker's face and in the immediate vicinity—including the milk bucket. We soon learned that it was wise to keep our mouth shut when this blow was delivered.

After delivering such a blow, cows were known to follow it up with additional applications, which did nothing to increase the milker's sense of security. We were forced to speed up the milking process to the point where our hands became a blur, but the small size of the spigots involved placed limits on this increase. Meanwhile, we kept our eye on the tail of the beast to the rear. Whenever she began to crank up for another blow, we would duck, but invariably the cow had anticipated this and aimed her blow slightly lower, hitting the back and saturating even more of our clothing.

When leaving the scene of such action, we appeared to have been dipped in a foaming septic tank, and we smelled the same way. Profanity was not permitted in English, and any words used in German were too mild to relieve the inner tensions we experienced.

KEEPING THE COW BARN CLEAN

Cleaning the cow barn was a daily chore. The brief time that the cows spent in the barn for milking in the summer did not normally lead to extensive manure being deposited, and whatever appeared was removed daily by taking a shovel and throwing it out on a pile through an open door or window. However, as previously noted, there were occasions when this waste acquired an undesirable degree of liquidity, which meant it could be found in every crack and crevice of the barn walls. Scraping it off was not always effective and in many cases it was better to let it dry and remove the crust later. Needless to say, when in the cow barn under such conditions, no one dallied behind cows when their tails began to rise.

In the winter, when the cows and other nonmilking cattle were in the barn most of the day, cleaning the barn became a more formidable task. A well-designed cow barn has a trench built into the floor effectively positioned behind the stanchioned cows so that their waste would fall in it. A shovel the width of the trench was used to remove the waste. Our cow barn at Ledyard did not have a trench and the cows frequently ended up standing in their own waste for extensive periods of time. The other cattle, not in stanchions, deposited their waste at random anywhere in the cow barn, and they and their waste had to be removed before milking began. Straw bedding was put around the cows every evening and this absorbed some of the liquid and provided tensile strength to the waste. A manure fork was then used for removal.

Modern barns had manure carriers that were metal containers suspended from an overhead track. Manure was placed in these containers, and they were pushed along the track to the outside where they were dumped, depositing their contents on the manure pile. Of course, we had no such facility and it was necessary to carry every shovel or forkful to the door or window and throw the manure out on the pile, which was not far from the door or window.

SEPARATING AND DISPOSING OF MILK PRODUCTS

When I became old enough to milk, I also inherited the job of separating. A brief look at this process may be of interest.

The specific gravity of butterfat is less than the other ingredients in milk. If milk is not homogenized and is left to stand for some period of time, the fat globules will rise to the top where they can be skimmed off. (Homogenization breaks up the fat globules and the resulting smaller particles remain in suspension longer, making separation more difficult; people in town could not pour off the top of the milk bottle to obtain cream.)

The cream separator used this difference in specific gravity to separate the cream from the rest of the milk by subjecting the milk to a high centrifugal force in a bottle-shaped bowl that spun at a very high speed. This bowl was approximately six inches in diameter and contained many cone-shaped plates with the small end of the cones up. A crank on the side of the machine was used to bring the bowl up to speed and maintain the speed during separation. Because the bowl was quite heavy and the gear ratio high, several minutes were required to bring it up to speed. A bell near the handle of the crank would ring until centrifugal force from the turning crank prevented it from ringing when the bowl was up to the desired speed and separating could commence. Inertia kept the bowl spinning freely for many minutes after separation had ceased.

The milk was poured through a funnel containing a filter and was released from the tank at the top of the separator into a float chamber that controlled its flow into the spinning bowl. At first a fine screen was used for a filter. Later, paper filters were used and they did a better job of removing the fines. Although few of the bacteria were pathogenic, they could still pass through. No doubt pasteurization killed most of the bacteria for those who lived in town.

On entering the bowl, the milk was immediately forced to the outside by centrifugal force, and the cream, being lighter, was forced to the center and upward where it exited through a small orifice into a spout and emptied into the cream container. The skim milk, being heavier, exited through a larger orifice at a lower elevation into its own spout and container.

In warm weather milk proved to be a good medium for the reproduction of bacteria and this dictated the need to clean the separator daily during the summer. Traces of milk remained confined in the small spaces between the plates in the bowl, and a special wrench was used to loosen a nut at the top of the bowl so the plates could be removed and individually cleaned with soap and hot water. The plates were then strung on a wire holder to dry. All the parts had to be reassembled for use that evening.

Because we did not drink milk, whole milk was never taken directly to the house. Small amounts of cream and skim milk were used for cooking, cereal, coffee, and such. The main portion of the skim milk was fed to the calves and the hogs. Cream was kept in a cool place until it could be taken to the creamery. Some farmers had a covered tank near their well where the water was used to keep cream cans cool, but we had no such facility.

It should be noted that since they sold cream, which contained butterfat, farmers were partial towards butter and the use of margarine was not popular. State law did not permit the sale of margarine that was colored like butter, so a small plastic tube containing coloring was placed in each package for the customer to mix and make the margarine look more like butter.

HOUSEWORK

It should be made clear that chores were not the exclusive domain of the male members of the family. The role women played in washing clothes with primitive facilities, hanging out the wash in freezing weather, and ironing the entire batch using irons heated on the kitchen range is well known, but the magnitude of other tasks such as obtaining and preparing sufficient food for a relatively large family with healthy appetites and keeping the house clean and comfortable is often overlooked. Although I am incapable of adequately noting their role, simple justice demands a few comments.

Mother's first task in the morning was stoking the kitchen

range. It took considerable time for the fire to heat the heavy iron stove plates and the cast iron utensils. While the stove was heating, Mother and Dolores went to the barn to do their milking before they prepared breakfast.

All food had to be ready to serve when the men came in from chores and had washed up. The procedure was the same for all meals—when all were seated at the table, we quietly bowed our heads and Dad said grace.

Meals were simple and our appetites were always good. In addition to various hot and cold cereals, breakfast included thin crepelike pancakes, eaten with a generous topping of syrup. Dinner, served at noon, and supper invariably included our staples— potatoes, homemade bread, and meat or its substitute, eggs. Coffee was served with all meals, and frequently we had a dessert of sauce or pie.

Mother used the usual methods of food preparation and supplemented them with a few unique approaches of her own. No doubt the preparation of meat dishes gave the women the greatest difficulty; beef steak, tenderized by pounding with a special hammer made for this purpose, pork chops, chicken, and such were easy to serve, but were frequently in short supply. When this was the case and the usual egg substitute had made a sufficient number of appearances, Mother turned to meatloaf.

The word "meatloaf" was used to describe any dish that utilized ground meat as one of its ingredients. The meat's fat content no doubt approached 100 percent and was purchased for as little as eight cents a pound; soda crackers were used to expand its volume. Much of the fat was absorbed by the crackers, making them taste more like meat, and the residue of meat gave a distinctive meatlike appearance to the mixture. The amount of crackers added was directly proportional to the number of people to be served, and Mother could miraculously expand a pound of hamburger into a meatloaf sufficient to feed any number of people. She was a firm believer in the biblical story of the loaves and fishes, and I suspect she came quite close to duplicating this feat.

We raised most of our vegetables, eating them fresh in season and canned in winter. Occasionally, Mother would purchase a small can of corn or peas, which meant restraint was required when taking a helping. Creamed corn required the use of crackers to enlarge the amount available. Here again, she had the ability to expand the dish to serve any number of people. Crackers must have rivaled flour in the quantity purchased.

Oil cloth was used as a covering for the kitchen table, and a tablecloth was used when our infrequent formal dining took place in the living room. In the winter, when the heating stove occupied a prominent place along the north wall of this room, expansion of the dining room table to its full size involved extensive advance planning.

Several factors made cleaning house a never-ending task. Although overshoes were left at the door, the entry of dirt on shoes was not unknown, and work clothes that had been worn for a week in a dust-laden environment were not reluctant to release some of their contamination in the house. During dry windy weather, especially during dust storms, extremely fine airborne soil found entry into the house less than challenging and its removal was not done with the use of a vacuum cleaner. Mother's high standards of cleanliness led to our linoleum floors being scrubbed harder and more often than those of us who treaded upon them. In extremely cold weather, washing the kitchen floor was difficult because the warm wash water would cool and freeze before it could be mopped up.

Houses were for humans and all forms of animal life were discouraged as inhabitants. Because fly spray added an undesirable seasoning to food, we did not use it in the house. However, we did use it at the entrance and on the porch. Some families used flypaper strips that hung from the ceiling, attracting flies to their sticky coatings. Eating a meal at a table that had a flypaper strip, generously coated with dead flies, hanging above it was not a setting we preferred, and this means of insect control was never used.

Bed bugs were discovered in an upstairs bedroom the day we moved into the Ledyard house and their departure received the highest priority. Pesticides were not readily available, so Mother used kerosene. It was generously dispensed from an oil can to all conceivable hidden places in the floor boards, the baseboard, the bed frame, and springs. Our bedroom soon smelled like a refinery, which no doubt convinced any surviving bugs that moving was a prudent course of action. Fortunately, this kerosene never became a source of fuel for a fire. The use of open flames in our kerosene lamps made this a possibility, and such a fire would certainly have resulted in a most spectacular blaze.

Mother was always concerned about having enough covers on the beds. Although summer was no problem, winter was a different matter. Wilbur and I generally occupied the north bedroom; this room did not receive heat of any kind. Although Dad would get up in the middle of the night to stoke the heating stove, its warmth did not reach our room. To make matters worse, one of the window panes had a corner missing, and because there were no storm windows upstairs, we placed a rag in the opening to keep out the elements. During a blizzard, snow would frequently accumulate on the sill.

Keeping warm under these conditions required considerable forethought. The bed covers included flannel sheets, regular blankets, quilts, and on the very top, the buffalo robe. When going to bed we undressed in the living room down to our long underwear (we never had pajamas) made a mad dash up the stairs, tunneled under this pile of bedding (whose weight approached the limits of human endurance) and assumed a fetal position. When blood began to circulate again in our outer extremities, we made a small opening through the bedding to permit the entry of fresh air. There were numerous mornings when I found frost from my breath on the buffalo robe around the fresh air opening.

We did not have hot water bottles, but occasionally Mother would heat one of her irons, wrap it in a towel, and we would carry this to bed to keep our feet warm. Although the irons felt good when going to bed, in the morning their icy presence made them undesirable bed companions.

When I Wasn't Doing Chores

Although chores were a part of my life beginning at a very early age, there was sufficient time during nonschool hours to pursue recreational pursuits, especially before I was old enough to work in the field at age twelve.

RECREATIONAL FACILITIES

A large cottonwood tree near the house had a limb at just the right height for a swing, but it had to be shared with Dolores. I had a few small toys such as a tractor, plow, truck, Spirit of St. Louis airplane, and a sled, but economic conditions soon prevented acquisition of the larger variety. The gifts we received at Christmas seldom exceeded the price of one dollar, and birthdays were not an occasion for receiving superfluous items such as toys. I had some small wagon parts, but I was never destined to have a new one, and our home was never blessed by the presence of a tricycle.

I understood that money was in short supply and seldom pressured Dad for expensive things, but there was one occasion when a used bicycle caught my eye in the hardware store and my restraint came unleashed. The $3.95 price was unusually low and I attempted to convince Dad that such a bargain should not be permitted to escape. The price was indicative of its condition, and no doubt he made the correct decision in not buying it. We never found an acceptable bicycle with an affordable price tag.

Since large store-bought items were not available, it was necessary to make my own. Dad had a complete set of hand-operated tools and he did not object to Wilbur or me using them provided we operated and took care of them properly. He provided very little instruction for their use, so we learned by watching him and proceeding on our own by trial and error. There was little danger in the use of most of them, but a few, like the blowtorch, had to be operated with care.

Building materials, such as used lumber, round and rectangular steel bar stock, steel pipe, and junk, consisting of old farm equipment, cars, and engines, were available, and with the hand-operated drill press and bolt and pipe dies, our ability to make things was greatly enhanced. The used lumber had come from the oats bin on the Lakota farm, which Dad had dismantled; he was given this lumber for erecting a new sheet metal bin. Extensive nails remained embedded in this lumber and they were removed, straightened, and reused. Although of dubious quality, many pleasant and constructive hours were spent in designing, building, and operating my homemade toys and machines.

PETS

A dog was a necessity on the farm and in our case it was also a pet. We always had one (only one), an uncastrated male. When we moved from Lakota to Ledyard, we kept him penned up in the barn for several days to become acquainted with his new home, but apparently he was not impressed by it and disappeared. It was only eight miles between the farms, so we looked for him along this route and at the old farm, but he was never seen again.

A shepherd was ordered from a place that advertised them for sale in the *Wallaces Farmer* magazine. This dog we called Shep. Because animals were not allowed in our house, Shep slept either in the barn during the winter or near the house at other times. Shep ate table scraps because there was no such thing as buying dogfood, and he never saw a veterinarian or received a shot. He was trained in an adequate (but unprofessional) manner to assist us in controlling other animals on the farm. He was not permitted to chase cars or bark excessively.

Our other animals did not fear Shep when he was not ordered to attack, and he could walk quietly among them, but when we told him to "sic em," they soon learned to respond quickly. Hogs were controlled by biting and hanging onto their ears, and he encouraged cattle to move along by biting their heels before stepping back while they took one more step to position themselves for a kick, which would always miss him. He learned this the hard way, by being kicked a few times. The cattle learned to fear him and they quickly pursued the direction of travel we wanted them to take. Shep was also good at catching roosters, and whenever Mother wanted one, we'd send him in pursuit.

Shep was a constant companion on my many hiking, trapping, and hunting excursions, some of which proved to be of great interest to me. On one occasion, we had just reached the edge of our gravel pit when we saw a skunk in the bottom heading for a hole in the opposite bank, apparently its den. Shep immediately went into the pit and approached the skunk from the front, and the skunk, thinking it an opportune time to expose its backside, appropriately maneuvered itself. At this point, events transpired so rapidly that it is not clear if the skunk delivered his unwelcome gift before Shep grabbed him, or shortly thereafter. In any case, the gift was delivered. Shep shook the skunk vigorously in his mouth a few times, threw it a few feet, and made a hasty retreat. The skunk was immobile and appeared to be dead; however, because the smell in the pit was so excessive, I made no attempt to verify the death.

Apparently, the discharge from a skunk is painful to a dog's nose, not only because of its smell, but also its toxic effect. Shep appeared to be in misery, rubbing his nose vigorously in the grass and snorting loudly all the way back to the farmyard, where Mother happened to be when we approached. We were at least a hundred feet from her and had said nothing when she shouted that I should take my clothes off outside, go in the house to wash up, and put on some different clothes. Shep was not welcome around the house for a few days and he seemed to understand why.

On another occasion, we were in the large pond when it was dry and encountered a black animal about the size of a cat. Shep immediately attacked and killed it. Not knowing what it was, I took it to Dad, who informed me that we had killed a mink. If this animal had been available in quantity during the winter, trapping could have proven profitable, but our farm did not provide a suitable year-round environment for mink.

When we moved to Manly, we took Shep with us and kept him in the barn for ten days until we thought he had adapted to his new home. However, such was not the case. He also disappeared and was never seen again.

Cats were needed around a farm to keep rats and mice under control and we always had several. When their numbers became excessive, small kittens were killed. The mothers generally had their kittens in a place hidden from view and it was a challenge for us to find them. The small, cuddly kittens were cute and received a great deal of attention from all of us—perhaps too much. Teaching them to drink from a pan or saucer, and later to take a stream of milk directly from a cow being milked, was a pleasant task. Although the adult cats were given milk in an old, handle-less scoop in the cow barn and received a few scraps of food from the house, they usually had to catch most of their own food. Cats have a natural inclination to catch birds, including small chicks. They had to be taught that chicken killing was forbidden. The cats that did not quickly learn this were destroyed.

WILDLIFE

Some of my fondest memories involve the extensive wildlife on our farm. Our large permanent pasture, the ponds, and our prairie hayland, provided safe nesting areas and a good environment for a variety of creatures. Pheasants were numerous, and in the spring we frequently heard the distinctive call of the cocks and saw fights between them for the favor of a hen. Nests containing their brown eggs were often located, and later the chicks would be seen with their mothers. Once I captured a few chicks and attempted to raise them, but they would not eat for me and soon died. Another time I took a few eggs from a nest and put them under a sitting hen, but they did not hatch. Perhaps they became too cold during the move. I was to have more experiences with pheasants later as a hunter.

Although Dad frequently spoke of prairie chickens, I do not recall seeing any of them. However, Hungarian partridges were occasionally encountered. They stayed in groups and when flushed, would fly off together. They are smaller than the ring-necked pheasant, and were reported to be good eating.

There were numerous birds around our farm, including sparrows, blackbirds, woodpeckers, owls, pigeons, crows, hawks, robins, canaries, mourning doves, killdeers, and others whose names I did not know. I learned to identify many of their eggs and frequently saw an adult feign injury to lure me away from its young. In the spring, migrating waterfowl would occasionally rest on our ponds. Unfortunately, because the ponds were dry in the fall during their return journey, we never saw them then.

We had a few pocket gophers and moles, but my first experience in trapping involved the numerous gophers (ground squirrels) we had in our pasture. I used the traps Wilbur had used at Lakota and found the single-spring ones particularly effective because the double-spring traps were too large for the entrance to a den. Ground squirrels are very inquisitive and would reappear again in a matter of minutes after entering their dens.

Cottontails and jackrabbits were plentiful, but Shep could not run as fast as the jackrabbit, and getting these animals had to wait until I hunted them with guns. However, Shep could catch a cottontail if it did not have a nearby shelter, such as a woodpile, and he would occasionally be successful. Depending on their age, small bunnies were easily caught. I attempted to raise a few, but they refused to eat and these attempts proved unsuccessful.

There was evidence of a badger on our farm, but it was never seen. I did see one that had been trapped on a relative's farm; it was a vicious-looking animal that was killed with a shotgun. Badgers are very aggressive when disturbed and must be approached with care. They were not one of our preferred species of wildlife.

On one occasion, I encountered a weasel that had killed one of our chickens. It had its mouth around the chicken's neck, apparently drawing blood. I took one of the chicken's legs and lifted it in the air, but the weasel remained attached until I shook the chicken vigorously. Instead of running away, which is what I expected, the weasel ran towards the dog to attack it. Fortunately, he chose the dog instead of me. I was rather surprised to see the dog temporarily back off, and the weasel made his escape. Although small, they are very aggressive and can inflict painful injuries.

Squirrels would occasionally make their appearance, but we had no nut trees and too many cats, so they did not make our farm a permanent home.

Two kinds of snakes were frequently seen: the bull and the

garden snake, both harmless to humans. We had no rattlesnakes. Because snakes eat rodents, they were beneficial to the farmer, but observing a snake swallowing a toad, larger in diameter than itself, was not a pleasant sight. Snakes were not my favorite wild animal. Although I never observed them in the shedding process, I periodically found their skins in the field.

Rats and mice were in evidence, but their numbers were controlled by our cats. An abandoned farmyard across the road and one-half mile south of us, where there was a pit silo with some remaining silage, illustrated what could happen when these rodents had an adequate food source and no predators to control them. One day when Shep and I happened to go into this pit, a rat ran out and was killed by Shep. In the process of chasing this rat, several others made their appearance and soon Shep was frantically involved in killing rats. Before we left, Shep had killed eighty and there were still many left.

Although our ponds dried up in the summer, they were home for several different kinds of wildlife. Crayfish would dig holes to the watertable below, depositing the removed soil at the surface of the ground. Frogs also found a livable environment. Croaking frogs and countless polliwogs were so much a part of our environment in the summer that this farm cannot be imagined without them.

HUNTING

Hunting comes naturally to some and such was the case with me. I started at a young age, using a homemade slingshot. A bow and arrow soon followed my slingshot days, and eventually I converted it into a crossbow with an attached sight. It was a formidable-looking weapon, but seldom has a weapon that looked so dangerous proven to be so ineffective. The sparrows and blackbirds I was allowed to hunt quickly developed disdain for my hunting prowess. As is so frequently the case, the planning and building of the bow proved to be more pleasurable than its use.

Lever-action BB guns could be purchased for $1.35, sufficiently close to the one-dollar Christmas limit, and I received my first one at age ten. My game, sparrows and blackbirds, quickly learned to maintain a respectful distance. I found the use of this weapon enjoyable; unfortunately, it didn't last through the year and we had to buy a new one.

Except for eyes, BB guns were not considered dangerous weapons. However, I was expected to treat mine as a dangerous weapon and did so except on one occasion. One day while strolling back through the pasture after an unsuccessful hunt, I passed by our herd of cattle, and that organ possessed only by the bull came to my attention. My lack of success at finding suitable targets that day led me to consider this one and I got off a fast shot. Being somewhat familiar with the sensitivity of this organ, I was not surprised at the bull's reaction and made a hasty retreat. Fortunately, the bull did not know the source of his discomfort and made no attempt to follow.

Close observation of the bull the next few days indicated no adverse effect on his performance, and a distant inspection of the organ did not uncover any unusual appearance. Apparently the impact of the BB was within the range the organ was designed to sustain.

I had reason to believe that Dad did not get me this gun to pursue this type of activity, and had he known that I had, I would have been punished. Needless to say, this target was left undisturbed.

A farm boy and a .22-caliber rifle are a natural combination, which proved to be the case with me. Such a gun cost more than I was allowed for Christmas and the ammunition was also more expensive, so Dad was rather reluctant to purchase one for me. However, I persisted and we looked at a single-shot that was for sale in the hardware store at Lakota for $3.95. Dad was not impressed with it, so I concentrated on the catalogs.

There were two guns in the catalog that appealed to me: a Remington bolt-action single-shot that sold for $5.95 and a Remington bolt-action repeater that had an $8.95 price tag. The cost of the repeater was too much, but finally Dad said that if I stayed out of school for one week and helped him pick corn by hand, he would get me the single-shot for Christmas. Although I did not enjoy picking corn by hand, this was an offer I could not refuse and on Christmas morning, a Model 33 Remington bolt-action, single-shot .22 was lying on the dining room table with a box of ammunition. My hunting horizon was about to expand dramatically.

Training courses for hunting safety were unknown and Dad's only instructions were to keep the barrel pointed up into the air, unless I was shooting at something. Observing the background of the target before shooting, keeping in mind that a .22 bullet will travel an extensive distance, was also stressed. Dad made sure that I knew the purpose of the gun's safety. Loaded guns were not permitted in the house.

A box of fifty .22 shorts cost twelve cents, unless I could find them on special for ten cents. This was the only ammo I was to use because the long or long rifle shells cost sixteen cents a box, an unnecessary expense. Obviously, with the cost of this ammo I could not shoot as frequently as I could with the BB gun, and my targets had to be picked with care. My work now included more chores and work in the field, so I had less free time, but when time permitted, hunting became my chief pastime.

Sparrows and blackbirds were still targets, but other larger animals were added to the list, including gophers, which I hunted instead of trapped. A gopher's inquisitive habit of sitting upright at the entrance to a den and making a distinctive sound made an ideal target for me while in a prone or sitting position. The gun could not be loaded by placing a shell directly in front of the bolt and pushing the bolt forward; the shell had to be put directly into the chamber, which was somewhat time-consuming and prevented quick second shots. I soon learned to make the first shot count.

Cottontail rabbits could be approached quite closely, when they thought they had not been observed. It wasn't long before I shot my first rabbit, and after skinning it out, I brought it to Mother for cooking. She refused to prepare it, saying something about rabbit fever. Mother also made it clear that jacks were on the forbidden list. I was not upset by her decision because a produce dealer in Lakota purchased frozen, unskinned and undressed jacks for ten cents, and cottontails for five cents. Selling the rabbits gave me the opportunity to make money for buying more ammo. I was told that these rabbits were shipped to Chicago, where the skins were probably used, but whether the meat was used is unknown.

The jack would never permit Shep and me to make a close approach. However, when a jack was flushed Shep's natural instinct was to run after it, even though he knew he could never catch it. I soon found that jacks were curious animals and if Shep and I both remained in a stationary position, the jacks stopped, sat on their haunches in an upright position, and watched us.

Although they were quite some distance away, they still became good targets.

Shep was taught to stay at my side. When a jack jumped up, I would get into a kneeling position and wait for curiosity to take command of the jack's actions. After correcting for wind and distance, a carefully placed shot would follow. From the jack's reaction and the sound of the bullet's impact, a hit was soon obvious, and Shep automatically ran towards the wounded jack, having no difficulty running it down.

My attachment to the .22 continued, even after the shotgun joined my arsenal. Although it took a subordinate role for hunting, I continued to use the .22 for target practice and plunking.

My introduction to the use of a shotgun was a dramatic one. Dad had a twelve-gauge Remington semiautomatic with the Browning movable barrel patent, which he had purchased wholesale for eighteen dollars when he owned the hardware store in Kamrar. My first use of this gun began without the benefit of any kind of instructions. It was during pheasant hunting season when Dad, casually and without notice, told me to get the gun. While Mother was watching, he told me to load the gun because he was getting ready to toss a can into the air for me to shoot.

This gun has a safety, a small trigger located immediately in front of the regular trigger, and when it is back, the large trigger is inoperable. Having observed its use many times by Dad and Wilbur, I knew how it worked, but I proceeded to load the gun *before* securing the safety, and when I reached down to put it in place, I inadvertently pulled the main trigger. Fortunately, the gun was pointed away from Dad and Mother and no harm resulted, but the gun flew out of my hand and Mother, who became very excited, wanted to stop the whole affair. Dad said he was glad this happened since no harm was done and I quite obviously had learned a good lesson. He told me to reload, and after I did so he tossed the can into the air. It wasn't long before I joined the big boys, bringing home pheasant for the pot, but I never again loaded the gun without checking the safety first.

After its introduction into our country, the ring-necked pheasant found the Midwest an ideal environment, and during the 1920s and 1930s, sufficient ground shelter and food was available for them to propagate profusely. The daily bag limit per hunter during the hunting season was seven, including three hens. Even with such high limits, there was a period during the early thirties when their numbers became excessive.

As noted on page 94, farmers during the 1920s and 1930s checked most of their corn. In this method of planting, several kernels were planted together in what was called a hill of corn, with the hills located forty inches apart. Pheasants had the uncanny ability of being able to locate these hills before the corn came up without the necessity of scratching around at random to find them. They went directly from hill to hill eating the seed that had been planted. Using the hand planter, we replanted some of these hills, but because this corn was planted later, it did not always mature, so replanting did not prove to be an acceptable solution. Control of the pheasant population was obviously the only practical course of action, and under these circumstances, it is my understanding that farmers had the right to shoot pheasant out of season, providing they did not keep them. Dad proceeded to do so, giving them to a Mexican family who worked for our neighbors to the south.

My father had enjoyed hunting when he was young, and we have pictures of him and a few companions with some game they shot, including a wolf that was later mounted and kept in the hardware store. For many years he permitted strangers to hunt on his farm. However an unfortunate experience led him to change this policy.

A group of men from Des Moines had been hunting on our farm for several years. One year when they came hunting, our picker was sitting in the field because Dad had decided to finish the picking by hand. They had been told not to hunt in the un-picked fields because the ears on the open-pollinated corn were easily knocked off. Not heeding Dad's request, the men were hunting in the same field where he was picking corn. A pheasant was flushed near Dad and some of the pellets from the resulting shot struck Bess, one of the horses. The physical injury to the horse was not serious, but she became emotionally upset and Dad had a very difficult time controlling her and calming her down. (See page 121.) To add fuel to the fire, Dad discovered two wrenches from the toolbox on the picker were missing. After that incident, Dad permitted no hunting on our farm unless he knew the hunters personally.

The severe 1935–1936 winter proved to be a disaster for pheasants and their numbers were drastically reduced. Hunting that fall, and later at Manly, never proved to be as good as before. The pheasants lost more and more of their ground cover and this kept their numbers from returning to the previous level.

As a youth I enjoyed hunting a great deal, but this activity no longer enthralls me. Age brings our mortality into clearer focus and this enhances our respect for all life. Some of our wildlife such as rodents had to be controlled and their demise by trap or gun was no less humane than their departure in the jaws of a predator or by slow starvation. In any case, proper training and respect for all governing regulations should be a prerequisite for the right to pursue this activity.

OTHER FORMS OF RECREATION

A boy sitting on a bank beside a body of water and holding a fishing pole while staring at a bobbing cork was a role I was seldom to play, and never successfully. The dredge ditch a mile east of us, which may not have contained any fish, was too difficult to get to, and there were no other fishing spots nearby. On only two occasions was I to go fishing, both times with Wilbur.

The first time was when we lived at Ledyard and Wilbur took me along with him to a lake in Minnesota where we fished from the bank. Wilbur used a cane pole, which was used on the binder as a whip, and I used a long stick. With worms for bait and corks for floats, we spent a peaceful day gazing at our corks that never bobbed.

The second occasion was when we lived at Manly and Wilbur decided to go first class. We went to Clear Lake and rented a rowboat for fifty cents. Using the same equipment we had used before, we spent another peaceful day staring at corks but seeing no signs of life.

It was difficult for me to understand how the fishing written about in *Sports Afield* could be so successful and ours so bad. I was never destined to catch a fish, or even have a bite, until years after I left home.

I know of no manmade swimming pools in existence near our home. Those communities near a lake needed no such facility, while many others without lakes had gravel pits deep enough to contain water during most of the year. Unfortunately, our community had neither one; our gravel pit and ponds were much too shallow and dried up in hot weather. My only opportunity to go swimming was when we went to a lake on the Fourth of July or went on our Sunday school picnic. Both were insufficient for me to learn how to swim.

Our ponds seldom contained water in the winter, so ice skating was not an activity frequently enjoyed. When the opportunity did present itself, I used our clamp-on skates. Again my limited participation did not lend itself to the acquisition of any techniques of an admirable nature.

Trains fascinated me and on a few occasions I walked to Gerled a mile south of our farm to observe them up close. Here the Rock Island railroad crossed over the Chicago and North Western railroad tracks by means of a viaduct and trains on the CNW tracks below could be viewed from above. There was no railroad station at Gerled so trains did not stop unless flagged, and stories about people being caught on a railroad bridge when a train approached made me cautious. On one occasion, a locomotive became snowbound on the CNW tracks, and its release a day later became an occasion for nearby residents to observe rescue procedures.

We received the *Des Moines Register* by mail every day except Sunday and it was a source of reading for all of us. I recall a few subjects such as the Lindbergh kidnapping trial and Will Rogers' fatal plane crash, but my primary interest was the comic page.

My parents also subscribed to *Wallaces Farmer,* the *American,* and *Sports Afield* magazines, as well as several religious publications. *Sports Afield,* received for my benefit, provided me with information on large-caliber rifles, and when in the hardware store, I would look at the gun rack to see if I could recognize any that had been discussed or advertised.

Our Fada radio was a source of entertainment for all when a power source was available. Three different kinds of batteries were required for its operation and they were referred to as A, B, and C batteries. The two-volt A battery provided current for the tube cathodes, the two forty-five-volt B batteries were connected in series to provide the ninety volts required on the tube anodes, and the low-voltage C batteries provided the bias voltage to the tube grids. Originally, dry cells were used for all, but later one cell of a six-volt car battery was used for the A battery because it was the one that went dead first and a car battery could be recharged. There were even occasions when we parked the car close to the house so we could connect the car battery without removing it from the car.

This radio did not have heterodyning nor were its tuning condensers ganged, and it was necessary to tune in, or set, three different dials to the correct setting before a station could be received. Since stations were few in number, this tedious method of locating stations did not prove to be an obstacle. During the latter years at Ledyard, we could seldom afford batteries, but when we could, I recall listening to WNAX, Yankton, South Dakota, KFNF Shenandoah, Iowa, and WHO, Des Moines, Iowa.

Working in the Field

INTRODUCTION TO FIELDWORK

The proper performance of fieldwork required not only the ability to control horses or drive a tractor, but also sufficient maturity to act in a rational manner when the unexpected happened, which was not infrequent. Doing such work was definitely a milestone for those of us growing up on the farm. My first fieldwork experience involved our four-section drag, a spike-tooth harrow.

Each section of this implement was approximately four feet wide and, when in use, made a swath about sixteen feet wide. This is wider than most gates, so it had to be disassembled, loaded into a wagon with the eveners, taken to the field, and reassembled. Four horses were used to pull it, and when I first began operating this implement, it had no place for the operator to ride, which meant that I had to walk on the soft ground behind, breathing the dust-laden air.

Dad went with me to the field the first day to help me assemble the implement and get started. He returned home while I proudly strutted down the field. When I reached the end and began to turn around, I realized the drag was too close to the fence. At least sixteen feet from the fence is required for the four sections to pivot around one end. Unfortunately, I was closer than this. Because a drag has no tongue and cannot be backed, I had to unhitch the horses, completely disassemble the implement, and reassemble it again in the correct location. Fortunately, no one was around to observe this faux pas, but my confidence was severely shaken.

As work proceeded, the cloud of dust I was walking in soon coated the inside of my nose, making it necessary for me to periodically use my handkerchief to remove the accumulation of mud. The dust wasn't my only difficulty; the soft ground made walking difficult and I became tired, but of course there was no thought of slowing down or stopping—after all, I was now a man. When noon arrived, the horses were unhitched in the field and I staggered home behind them.

My walk to the field after dinner was less spirited than it had been that morning; the afterglow from the step I had taken to maturity did not seem as warm and attractive as I had expected it to be. As the afternoon progressed, the thought of being a man seemed less appealing and great effort was necessary to finish the day. My chores that evening were not performed with much enthusiasm, and the pain in my legs frequently interrupted my sleep that night.

I soon toughened into the requirements of the job, and fortunately, it was a task quickly performed. Later, Wilbur made a two-wheeled cart from the remains of our buggy and attached it to the eveners of the drag, which meant we could ride. This eliminated the walking, but not, of course, the dust problem.

The next farm implement I was to operate was the single-row corn cultivator. This had a seat for the operator, and although legs and arms were required to maneuver the shovel gangs, it was not as fatiguing as walking. From this implement, I proceeded to the others used on our farm.

SOWING SMALL GRAIN

In the spring the fields remained frozen or muddy until the frost went out of the ground. Once the frost was gone, the fields quickly dried and fieldwork could begin. The first crop receiving our attention was oats. Before sowing, the seed oats had to be cleaned using a hand-operated cleaner to remove weed seeds such as mustard that had not been removed by the threshing machine. When a sufficient amount of oats had been cleaned and the ground could be worked, disking began in preparation for sowing.

We had two disks, an eight-footer that we no longer used and a ten-footer. Each was designed to be pulled with horses—four on the eight and five on the ten. These implements, similar to those now in use, consisted of a series of sharp-edged metal disks whose cutting edge cut into the ground a few inches when moved at an angle to the direction of travel. The disk would cut up corn stalks, dislodge root systems of corn plants, cut sod into small pieces, and break up large lumps of soil. They had a metal seat attached to a metal spring support that permitted limited movement in the vertical direction. When the disk was operated on rough ground, it was not unusual for the operator to be vigorously moved from side to side as well as up and down.

Early spring disking for oats generally took place in last year's corn crop. The hills and root systems left by this crop provided an ideal surface to toughen up the back and kidneys for the more strenuous rides we would experience later when disking newly plowed ground, especially if the new area was sod. Riding this bucking bronco would have been easier standing up so our legs could be used as shock absorbers, but unfortunately, this was not possible because the hand levers immediately in front of the seat did not permit adequate space for a standing platform. Because there was no pommel to hang on to, we had no choice but to keep our derrieres firmly planted on the hard, unpadded metal seat and perform a delicate balancing act. Safety was extremely important because falling in front of this implement, while it was moving, would prove fatal.

The vigorous physical motions did little to keep us warm during the cold days we had at this time of the year. Regardless of how many clothes we put on, they were never enough and at the end of the day, our cold-induced rigor mortis made dismounting difficult.

Seeding took place after the ground had been disked twice. Drilling and broadcast were the two different methods of seeding small grain. We, as well as most of our neighbors, used the broadcast system. This method used a mechanism that was attached to the tailgate of a wagon, and it uniformly cast seed over the ground. A large ring sprocket was bolted to one of the rear wheels and a chain from this sprocket powered the seeder as the team pulled the wagon forward. The operator would shovel seed oats from the wagon into a large hopper on top of the seeder. A smaller hopper for the clover, alfalfa, or smaller grass seeds was also attached to the seeder when these seeds were sown with the oats. (Oats were a nurse crop for other crops; they grew rapidly in the stubble after the oats were cut. Legumes had to be inoculated before seeding to ensure that their root systems produced nitrogen; this was done by mixing microorganisms with the seed by hand. We were advised not to breathe too much of this material when doing so.)

The seeder mechanism fed seed from the two hoppers to the top of two rapidly spinning disks with angle-shaped radial spokes that used centrifugal force to broadcast the seed over a wide swath in back of the moving wagon. The rate of feed could be adjusted by the operator to provide the desired density of seed on the ground. After the grain had been sown, the field was disked again to cover the seed with soil.

PLANTING CORN

Soybeans were not yet known in our community and corn was our major crop. Plowing for corn began immediately after the oats were sown. We had four plows, three horse-drawn—a walking plow, a sulky, and a gang—and one three-bottom tractor plow.

All plows were basically constructed the same. The cutting edge, or share, was bolted to the end of a hook-shaped beam immediately in front of the moldboard, which was generally solid but could be slotted; a landslide was attached to the moldboard at the side of the furrow. A colter wheel was supported from the beam and was used to cut sod along the edge of the furrow. The share was placed at an angle and came to a round point in front. As the plow moved forward, the share cut the soil at the bottom of the new furrow and the moldboard, immediately behind, turned it over into the previously made furrow. This action resulted in a horizontal thrust that was resisted by the landslide against the side of the new furrow. The cutting edges of shares tended to erode. They were either replaced with a new one or repaired in the blacksmith shop by depositing more metal on the cutting edge.

The walking plow was only used in the garden, where it could get into the corners and close to the fence. It had one bottom but no wheels and was moved about by laying it on its side and dragging it along the ground. Although we always used two horses, it could be pulled with only one. The operator walked behind with hands on the handles and reins around the shoulders. This plow required a great deal of physical effort to control, so Dad was naturally the one to operate it.

The sulky was also a single-bottom plow, but it had wheels and a seat for the operator. It was pulled by three horses, one walking in the previously made furrow and two on unplowed ground. The beam was raised by the operator's weight through a foot-operated lever, and a trip was used to drop it down again. There were two hand-operated levers to control the depth of plowing.

The gang plow was similar to the sulky except it had a gang of two bottoms and required five horses—side-by-side, not tandem—to pull it. One horse walked on previously plowed ground, one in the last furrow, and three on unplowed ground. Since it had two bottoms, plowing progressed more rapidly and it was the one we used when enough horses were available.

Tractor plows were constructed and performed much the same as horse-drawn plows, except they were controlled from the tractor instead of the plow. Hand levers projected forward and were within reach of the tractor operator. A trip rope was used to activate a mechanism that was geared to one of the plow wheels and raised the gang as the plow moved forward. This wheel had knobs on it to prevent it from sliding along the ground while raising the gang. The trip rope was also used to drop the gang for plowing.

Plowing was not an unpleasant task for the operator, except for those instances where the plow would not scour. When the plow was operating properly, soil moved smoothly over the moldboard to rest upside down in the previously made furrow, but occasionally when the plow had not been used for some time, soil would stick to the surface of the moldboard and not scour, interfering with the process. The operator had to stop the plow, raise the gang, and remove the soil from the moldboard surface by using a stick or foot, which was time-consuming. If scouring became a problem and if it was convenient, we polished the moldboard surfaces by briefly plowing in the gravel-filled soil surrounding our gravel pit. When plows were to be left unused for more than a day or two, the moldboard surfaces were coated with used machine oil, and if they were to be unused for longer periods, we coated the moldboard surfaces with grease or paint.

Plowing required extensive power and was hard work for the

horses. They needed numerous rest periods and those walking on plowed ground had to be watched closely for evidence of excessive fatigue. Plows took a smaller swath through the field than other implements, which meant it took longer to plow a field. It was no accident that the first use of tractors in the field was for plowing. However, because our Hart Parr tractor was no longer used for fieldwork when I began working in the field, my first experiences involved horses exclusively.

After the ground was plowed, it was double disked. This activity has been previously discussed and the degree of torture the operator experienced depended on the ground that had been plowed. The worst disking that I remember was on an original prairie that had just been plowed and looked like it was covered with large black leather strips. The sod resisted disk penetration, subjecting the disk to unusually large gyrations when moving on a diagonal. The horses also found the disking of plowed ground difficult and unpleasant. They could sink no lower as a beast of burden than to walk on such a surface while pulling such a heavy load.

After disking, the drag was used to break up the larger clods of dirt and smooth the ground for the planter. This operation was generally done twice; first in the direction of planting, the long direction of the field, and the last perpendicular to the first. It was important that the last one be perpendicular to the direction of planting because the planter used a marker to guide the operator in spacing the corn rows and this marker left a scratch mark on the ground in the direction of travel similar to that left by the teeth of the drag. It would be difficult to distinguish between them if they both went in the same direction.

There were a few occasions where additional fieldwork was required before the drag operation. A couch grass weed we called "quack grass" was present in most north Iowa farms. Its extensive creeping rhizomes thrived in cool, wet weather, and ground that was plowed in the fall was especially vulnerable to its growth. Normal field operations generally kept it under control, but a late, cold spring would require the use of the quack drag, or spring-toothed harrow. This implement did not have a seat for the operator and the task proved to be a slow, torturous one.

There was one other operation that was occasionally performed before using the drag. If the ground was exceptionally dry when plowed in the spring, the dirt clods were large and hard and the drag had difficulty breaking them up. Since they made planting more difficult, an implement we referred to as a pulverizer, or roller, was then used to reduce their size. Time seldom permitted extensive use of this implement.

Seed corn was obtained from our own crop. Dad removed choice ears from the wagons during corn picking and placed the ears in a protective environment to dry. Before the ears were put through the hand sheller, the larger butt kernels and smaller tip kernels were removed by hand. Seed corn had to be uniformly graded for the plates in the planter so that the correct number of kernels would be placed in each hill. There were grading machines made for this purpose, but we did not have one. The seed was then ready for testing.

It was important to determine how well the seed would germinate before planting, and this was done by using a large shallow metal tray, divided into small squares approximately one inch in size. A kernel of corn was placed in each square, water was added and the tray kept in a warm place in the house. The kernels would begin to sprout in a few days and the number of kernels that germinated out of one hundred was the percentage of germination. This provided a guide as to the quality of each batch of seed corn.

The planting of corn was a very critical operation that Dad reserved for himself. Because corn needed a long enough growing season to reach maturity before the first frost, which could be expected in northern Iowa any time after the middle of September, Dad would plant on or as close to the first of May as possible.

There were two methods of planting corn, drilling and checking. Drilled corn was used as fodder and the kernels were planted individually in a row a few inches apart. This resulted in rows of plants that could only be cultivated in the direction of planting. Checked corn consisted of several plants located together in what we referred to as a hill of corn. The planter located these hills so that they were in line in the lateral direction as well as the direction of planting and they could be cultivated in both directions. To insure alignment in the lateral direction a checking wire had to be used.

This wire consisted of segments forty inches long, which was the distance between rows and the distance between the planter wheels, joined together with a knot. The wire was wrapped around a spool and placed in the field by the planter with the operator carefully controlling the speed of the spool as the team moved the planter forward. When the wire was taken up, the planter rotated the spool and provided sufficient tension for the wire to be wrapped in a neat fashion.

After the wire had been placed along one side of the field in the direction of planting, the operator was ready to start the actual planting process. Dad had a two-row John Deere corn planter that operated similar to other planters then in use. The seed corn was placed in two containers, one for each row, on the planter. The bottom of the containers had plates that rotated a certain preset amount as the planter moved forward. There were recesses in the perimeter of the plates that a single kernel of corn would fall into as the plates slowly rotated. Different plates with different sized recesses were used for different sized kernels. (Later, plates were also obtained for planting soybeans.)

The planter had a control for setting the number of kernels desired in each hill (generally three or four), and as the planter moved forward the plates rotated just the right amount to drop this number on top of a trapdoor that was located below in the planter runner. The runner cut a small trench a few inches deep through the soil as the planter moved forward, and the knots on the checking wire, riding in a Y-shaped lever above, tripped the trapdoor as the knots went through the Y. The kernels on top of the door were deposited directly into the soil. The trapdoor quickly closed and the plates above again deposited the prescribed number of kernels on its top. The trapdoor had to be located immediately above the place the kernels were to be deposited so that there would be no delay when dropped. Any delay would deposit the kernels an inch or two forward, and on the return pass of the planter they would be deposited an inch or two in the other direction, causing a stagger in the corn row in the lateral direction, making it difficult to cultivate.

The checking wire was firmly staked down with steel stakes at each end of the field and as the planter approached the end, there was a lateral pull on this wire because the planter was now a few feet further away on its return pass. The operator would release the wire from the planter and after turning around, get off the planter, restake the end of the checking wire, and place it in the Y of the planter. (There was a Y-shaped tripping lever on each side of the planter.) Both sides of the planter had marker arms that were attached together by a rope, and as the planter was turned around, it pivoted about the marker that had just been used. This loosened the tension on the rope, permitting the marker on the other side to drop down while pulling the first marker up as it dug into the soil. The wheel of the planter followed the runners; their rims were shaped for pushing soil back into the small trench formed by the runner, covering the seed in the ground.

Corn needs a great deal of nitrogen for producing high yields. Because corn quickly reduced the quantity of nitrogen in the original prairie soil, crops were rotated. The use of inoculated legumes such as alfalfa was encouraged, but the main source for nitrogen renewal was manure. Because the quantity of manure was limited, other sources were soon sought. (Since horses produced manure and tractors didn't, some farmers were slow in embracing the use of tractors.)

Dad was one of the first in our neighborhood to use chemical fertilizers. The accessory needed to place the powder fertilizer in the ground near each hill was attached to the planter, and the planter mechanism triggered its placement when the kernels were dropped. Large containers for the fertilizer were located adjacent to the seed corn containers and they needed frequent refilling.

Unfortunately, his first use of this material during the dust bowl of the thirties did not prove satisfactory. It was an unusually dry year and much of the crop withered and died before maturity. Dad felt that the chemical fertilizer had contributed to this situation and he refused to use any chemical fertilizers again.

Corn destined to be put in silos was generally drilled and cut by a binder before it had matured and the leaves were still green. We were not to have a silo until later at Manly, but we used a small amount of our corn acreage for fodder for our cattle and this was drilled.

Drilling was a much simpler process than checking. The planter was set so that the plates rotated continuously at the rate required for the desired plant spacing and the trapdoor in the runner was left open. No checking wire was required and the planter operator did not have to get off the planter at each end. Since the corn was to be used for fodder, our plants were closely spaced, resulting in smaller ears but more digestible stems and leaves. This method of planting is now used exclusively. The many large fields of checked corn that were once visible alongside the roads can no longer be seen.

When the germinating corn was about to protrude through the ground, the field was dragged again to kill all the small weeds that had taken root in the interim. Cultivation began as soon as the corn rows could easily be followed by the cultivator operator.

We had two single-row and one double-row cultivators, all horse drawn. The two single-row cultivators were used for the first two cultivations, with Dad operating one and either Wilbur or I the other. The single-row cultivators consisted of two gangs of three shovels each, controlled by the feet and the hands of the operator. The shovels were kept in place by wooden pegs that would break when they struck a hard object like a rock, thus preventing damage to the shovel. The team of horses and the operator straddled the row being cultivated and shields were used during the first cultivation to prevent the small corn plants from being covered with dirt displaced by the shovels. The intent was to get the shovels as close to the hill of corn as possible without damaging or covering the corn. The shields offered less than perfect protection and when a hill was accidentally covered, it was necessary to stop and uncover it, which made the first cultivation a very time-consuming task.

The second cultivation, a cross cultivation, was done in the lateral direction and the corn was usually high enough so that shields were no longer required.

When the corn was approaching knee high, the third and last cultivations were done with the two-row cultivator in the direction of planting. The shovels were positioned to throw the dirt against the base of the corn stalks, covering any weeds that might surround them. This cultivation also had its unpleasant aspects because the early morning dew on the leaves would saturate our pant legs. Upon completion of the third cultivation, the crop was in the lap of the gods until harvest time.

MAKING HAY

Because large amounts of hay were consumed by our animals, the making of hay began in early summer and continued periodically until fall. Alfalfa was preferred, not only because of its quality, but also because three annual cuttings could be obtained from it. We had a few acres of alfalfa but it and the few acres of prairie were not sufficient for our needs. Additional sources were provided by small hay fields of red clover or timothy. Sweet clover (it does not taste sweet to humans—something I personally verified) was frequently used to supplement our permanent bluegrass pasture and when not fully grown, it made hay of acceptable quality. However, when mature, the stems were too large and tough.

The mower was a simple two-wheeled implement whose wheels were geared through a differential to a pitman arm that rapidly moved a five-foot sickle containing closely spaced V-shaped cutting blades that moved back and forth against shearing edges to cut the hay. It was not a difficult machine for a team to pull and except for oiling the pitman frequently, there was little for the operator to do. As a result, this task was a rather pleasant one. The newly mowed hay had a pleasing odor and when the last small portion of the field was being mowed, the reduced ground cover forced the field's animal residents to seek protection elsewhere, resulting in the exit of an unbelievable number of rabbits, pheasants, and various other forms of wildlife.

Hay was left to dry in the field before it was raked. If collected too soon, excessive moisture would cause it to spoil in the hay-mow or stack, and if left to dry too long, its most valuable element, the leaves, would fall off and remain in the field. A day or two in the sun was generally enough so that raking could proceed.

The rake was a two-wheeled implement with many semicircular tines that were approximately three feet in diameter and spaced a few inches apart. The tines collected the hay as they combed the ground. The rake was pulled with a team that found this task less than challenging. When a sufficient amount of hay had been collected in the tines, the operator activated a foot control and the wheels engaged a mechanism that raised the tines, leaving the enclosed hay in an elongated pile. On the next pass, the hay was placed adjacent to the previous pile forming a windrow. Hay loaders that were attached to the back of hayracks would be used to pick up the hay as they moved across the field along the windrow and deposit it in the hayrack. Because we did not have such an implement, we used the rake on the windrow to bunch the hay into piles or cocks. We used pitchforks to pitch it on the hayrack and it was then taken to the barn.

We did not have a hay carrier in the barn, so we had to unload the racks by hand. We would pitch it through a small door in the front of the barn where it would land on the roof of the milk room. Another man would move it back to the center of the barn, stacking it as high as he could reach. When the barn was full, or the pitching of hay became impossible, we made stacks in front of the barn.

Without a doubt, the making of hay was a physically demanding task. It was also a dirty one because hay contained much dust and when moved about, it released this dust to settle on the intruder. Masks were unknown and I recall feverish, allergic-type reactions after engaging in this activity.

HARVESTING SMALL GRAIN

Oats ripened in July and harvesting began by cutting and bundling the grain with a binder. Our grain binder was a McCormick Deering, a machine substantially more sophisticated than the one originally invented by McCormick. Its cutting mechanism was similar to that of the hay mower, but the sickle was longer and as the grain was cut, it was gently pushed onto a canvas-covered platform by a rotating reel. The canvas was on rollers and moved the cut grain to the right, where other canvases moved it up and into the bundling mechanism.

When the bundling mechanism contained enough grain to make a bundle, it automatically triggered the tying mechanism that bound the bundle with twine, tied the knot, and cut the twine free from one of the three spools of twine contained in a round holder near the operator's seat in back. The bundles were kicked onto a carrier rack, where they remained until the operator activated the carrier, dropping the bundles in windrows. There were controls to set the height of cut on the grain and the size of bundles to be made.

The binder was pulled by three horses, and a bull wheel under the main mechanism on the right side powered the binder mechanism. Since it was too wide to go through a normal farm gate when in the normal operating position, two additional wheels and a jacking mechanism were provided so these wheels could be placed under the heavy right end of the binder to permit its movement in the other direction. The tongue-and-pulling facility was then detached and placed at the left end of the implement, and it was pulled with the long dimension in the direction of travel.

Naturally, my father operated the binder. The first pass in the field was around the perimeter in a clockwise direction to get all of the grain close to the fence rows. Because the bundles were dropped in uncut grain, they had to be moved back near the fence line before normal cutting took place in the counterclockwise direction.

As Dad was doing the cutting, Wilbur and I followed the windrows, shocking the grain. Shocks were made by placing a bundle under each arm—heads of grain forward—and thrusting them forward and down with the tops leaning against each other. This process was repeated with four more bundles and then a single bundle was placed on top and spread out to protect the heads of grain in the bundles below. Although most farmers did not do so, Dad always insisted on capping his shocks.

Shocking grain bundles exposed our arms and the sides of our bodies to extensive abrasive action, and although Wilbur and I usually had our shirt sleeves rolled up, when shocking they were down. Even with sleeves down, our arms and sides became sore, particularly when shocking barley, which had beards of awned spikelets. Their sharp points were always aimed directly at our bodies and we received sharp jabs each time a bundle was placed under our arm. With a liberal application of salt from our sweat, the resulting wounds made the task a most unpleasant one.

Grain had to be cut and shocked when dry and a blazing sun was our constant companion. Our one-gallon sheet-metal-covered crock water jug was always an essential partner. It was filled with cool water from the well just before going to the field and it was covered and put under a shock to keep it out of the direct rays of the sun. Periodically, one of us would go back and bring it forward as we progressed around the field. Anna Marie would bring us a lunch at tea time, during the middle of the forenoon and afternoon; it included hot tea or coffee. These pleasant breaks offered us an opportunity to discuss the relative thirst-quenching merits of hot and cold beverages, while sitting on a bundle and getting a well-deserved rest. When Dad was finished with the cutting, he assisted us in shocking. Threshing was the next stage of harvesting grain.

Since we were no longer in the Lakota threshing ring, Dad purchased an old, wood-framed threshing machine so we could do our own. This machine had obviously been retired, and extensive repair was necessary before it could be used for threshing. The blower compartment, which projected back and over the rear wheels, had developed an excessive "old-age sag" and it was necessary to raise this part a few inches to prevent the making of an undesirable "wake" along the ground when the machine was moved.

Upon completion of these repairs, it was towed to the threshing site by the Hart Parr, belts were put in place, bearings were lubricated, the grain wagon was correctly positioned, and Wilbur and Dad got a load of bundles from the field. We were ready for action.

With Wilbur on the rack, Dolores on the grain wagon, and me tending the blower, Dad started the tractor and engaged the pulley. Unusual noises could be heard as the belts began to move the internal organs, and when it came up to speed, the machine's vibrations would have impressed a professional hula dancer. Painful groans were emitted as the machine swallowed the first bundles and intestinal growling indicated satisfactory digestion. Internal gas pressure seemed to be building up inside and dust and chaff began flying about when the blower at the rear suddenly exploded into action, discharging straw with the velocity of a hurricane. After a respectable pause, grain began to slowly flow from the top of the grain elevator into the wagon. The machine purred like a kitten as the old dowager relived a pleasant past.

Dad soon became involved in shaping the developing straw pile, indicating to me where he wanted the blower to deposit the straw. Dolores was watching the grain chute, making sure all went in the wagon and that it did not overflow. Wilbur remained busy pitching bundles. When the rack was empty, the tractor was stopped and the entire cycle repeated.

Although threshing machines were large, their operation was rather simple. Grain bundles were placed head first into the feeder, where they were conveyed towards several arms that used a chopping action to pull the bundles into the machine and cut the binder twine with cutting blades. The heads of grain were fed directly into a rapidly revolving main cylinder whose protrusions knocked the grain from the stems. The straw and grain were then expelled on top of the upper sieve, which shook the material and thrust the straw upwards and towards the back of the machine while the grain fell through the coarse sieve to a medium sieve below. The medium sieve continued this action, removing stems and other undesirable coarse material that had gone through the coarse sieve, while the grain fell to a fine sieve below. The fine sieve permitted small weed seeds like mustard to pass through and be disposed of while the grain continued on to the elevator that hoisted it up into a hopper. This hopper automatically dropped its contents when half a bushel of grain had been deposited into it. The grain was moved by various means into the grain wagon.

Measurement was by weight and was adjustable for different grains. In a threshing ring, farmers paid for use of the threshing equipment by the bushel and the number of bushels threshed was one-half the number of times the hopper had dropped its contents, which was recorded on a counter.

The tractor conveyed power to the thresher by a long belt that was attached to a pulley on the main cylinder of the machine. Other pulleys on this shaft conveyed power to other machine components by the use of flat belts because V-type belts were not then in common use. Whenever a portion of the machine became plugged or turned excessively hard, belts began to slip and were easily thrown, which was known as a fly off. Because the belts moved rapidly, it was not healthy for us to be in the vicinity when a fly off took place. Of course the machine had to be unplugged by hand, which was a time-consuming task. Belt tighteners were provided on the machine to keep them from slipping, but our belts were in their last years of old age and excessive tightening would result in breaking. A major repair was then necessary and required a metal belt splice. It was a task we did not seek. The most feasible solution was to use liberal amounts of belt dressing.

Belt dressing was a firm, black, sticky tarlike substance that came in cardboard tubes similar to our present caulking gun tubes. It was applied by peeling back some cardboard from one end and holding that end firmly against the inside of a moving belt where friction would cause it to get hot and melt, coating the inside of the belt. Because belts and pulleys are not respecters of hands and fingers, this had to be done with care. Fortunately, none of us was ever seriously injured.

The bearings of rapidly rotating shafts were lubricated with grease cups, and oil cans were used on the slower rotating ones. Each evening, all belts were loosened so they would not stretch excessively overnight. We had no machine shed, so our machinery was stored outside, and when not in use, belts were taken off and stored in a dry place.

Since straw provided bedding for farm animals, it was important to protect and keep it in a convenient place. Occasionally, farmers would have the thresher blow it into their barn, but generally it was put in a straw pile outside, which is what we did. The blower mechanism on threshing machines was designed so that the blower pipe could be manually moved in an arc, or it could be preset for the desired length of arc and put on automatic, where it would move the pipe slowly back and forth without human assistance. Because the automatic part of our machine was inoperative, I had to move it about manually. There was also an adjustment for the length of pipe desired and a control for the direction of discharge from the end of the pipe. The overall shape of the straw pile was determined by these controls; however, extensive hand dressing with a fork was still required.

Working on top of a straw pile as the thresher's blower was depositing straw was a very dirty job; Dad tied a handkerchief around his mouth like a mask to reduce the amount of dust he breathed. His appearance later provided ample evidence that this means of doing so was only partially successful.

We did our own threshing for several years, but an excessive number of breakdowns finally convinced Dad to retire the machine and join a local threshing ring. A closer look at this operation may be of interest.

When tractors began replacing the steam engine as a source of power, farmers began to band together to buy a thresher and power it with a tractor owned by one of them. This was the case with our threshing ring at Ledyard and later at Manly. A John Deere tractor, owned by John Drew, was our power source at Ledyard.

This ring operated much the same as the one we had been in at Lakota. There were two grain haulers (three when the grain had to be scooped off by hand) and several bundle haulers. At least three racks were needed to keep the machine in continuous operation when pitching from one side; pitching continuously from both sides required at least six. We were among the majority who provided a rack and team and pitched bundles. When there were people available who did not have a team, rack, or wagon, they were used as spike pitchers, assisting bundle haulers in the field in loading their racks.

The grain bundles had to be dry and it was important that only one bundle at a time enter the machine. (When heavy rains preceded threshing, the shocks were pushed over a day or so before, so that the bundles could dry out.) When pitching from both sides, a definite rhythm or beat would be established as the pitchers alternated. When a rack was empty, another full one would be waiting to take its place.

A convenient source of drinking water was necessary for the men, and if a well was not nearby, a cream can containing water, or perhaps buttermilk obtained from the creamery, was kept near the machine. A long-handled dipper was shared by all.

When dinner arrived, the men unhitched their teams, watered them, tied them to the back of their racks or wagons with a halter or a bridle with the bit removed, and gave them some bundles of grain to feed on. Some of the racks had feed boxes built on the back, otherwise the bundles were placed on the ground. The men proceeded to the house where wash basins, soap, and pails of water were waiting on wood stands outside, under a tree if available. After washing their hands and faces, the dirty wash water was cast aside and towels, which had to be shared, were used for drying.

Feeding threshers was a big operation. Some of the wives helped each other perform this task, but Mother's only assistance was Dolores and Anna Marie. Strenuous physical activity made the men hungry, and it was a matter of pride for the women to provide them with all of the wholesome, but not fancy, food they could eat. In addition to the usual potatoes and vegetables, two kinds of meat (beef was a necessity) were generally provided, a hot and cold beverage, and a dessert of pie. During the latter years of harvesting with threshing rings, some farmers took their threshers to a restaurant in town for this meal, relieving the women of this difficult task.

After dinner, there were a few moments of relaxation before work resumed. A lunch of cold meat sandwiches and hot coffee was provided during the middle of the afternoon.

When all the threshing had been completed, a thresher's meeting was held and accounts settled. Most of the rings were nonprofit because the threshing machine was collectively owned. For these rings the cost of operation, including the amortized thresher costs, were distributed among those in the ring. Because some farms were larger than others and provided two men, each farmer was given credit for the help provided and charged for the bushels of grain threshed. Occasionally, a keg of beer would be a guest at these meetings. Dad did not object to this but Mother did, so when beer was a part of the meeting, Dad did not attend.

A brief comment concerning fires should be noted here. We

experienced two potentially serious ones, both connected with threshing activities.

In 1936, while threshing at our place, Mother was using both cooking ranges; the one in the shanty overheated and set the roof on fire. I happened to be getting water at the well when she frantically asked me to get Dad, who was working on the straw pile. He immediately grabbed two buckets, filled them with water by dipping them into the stock tank, and dashed to the house.

The shanty was full of smoke, but flames could be seen on the ceiling around the stove pipe fiercely consuming the dry wood. Dad did not hesitate; he ran into the shanty and threw a bucket of water up and directly onto the fire. He staggered out, coughing from the toxic fumes, but immediately grabbed the other bucket and repeated the process. Fortunately, this retarded the fire enough so that the bucket brigade that the threshers had formed from the stock tank could put out the fire. There is no doubt that Dad's timely, but dangerous, action and the availability of help saved our house. However, this fire did not delay our meal. After the fire was out, the women continued their activities and the meal was served on time without any noticeable negative effect.

After we had finished threshing this same year, another ring, operating a mile south of us, was still threshing and had a fire. Apparently, a metal object had gotten into the blower where the blade struck it, producing sparks and igniting the straw. The straw pile burst into flames that spread so rapidly the tractor operator had to pull the machine away from the fire by pulling against the main belt.

They were threshing in an oat stubble field at the time and the burning straw pile ignited the stubble. A south wind quickly brought the fire to Highway 9, where it jumped the highway and ignited the field adjacent to us. This was Ed Donji's field; he got his tractor and plow and went into this field to make a firebreak. Unfortunately, he arrived too late, but because our grain had been harvested, our crop was not lost. Our corn fields to the east and north, which were still green, prevented further spread of the fire.

Immediately after threshing, cows were permitted to graze on fields of grain stubble, some of which contained a newly emerging clover crop. However, those fields where corn was to be planted next year were plowed near the end of summer before school began. This plowing reduced the amount that had to be done in the spring. Before going to school in the fall of 1936, I was to spend weeks on the sulky, plowing our burned field.

HARVESTING CORN

The corn binder had the appearance of a corn picker, but instead of removing the ears, it cut a single row of corn, binding it into bundles like the small grain binder. It was pulled by two horses and the bundles were dropped into windrows and shocked similar to small grain. Shocks were formed by placing two bundles together and stacking other bundles about them until there was a large enough number to provide stability to the shock, as shown in typical Halloween scenes. The bundles were kept quite small so they could be loaded onto a rack with a bundle fork. (Such was frequently not the case with bundles destined for the silo, especially if they contained sorghum.) Shocking corn was not pleasant, but the weather was cooler during this time of the year and the acreage involved was much less than our oats crop, so the task was soon completed.

When the bundles had dried sufficiently and time permitted, the hayrack was used to bring them to the farmyard to be stacked at a convenient place for feeding. Frequently, our workload did not permit this and we brought the shocks from the field as needed. It was not unusual for this activity to extend into the winter months when many of the bundle butts would be frozen to the ground and an axe was needed to free them. This task was performed many times during a blizzard. It should be noted that mice found these shocks a pleasant home with a built-in food supply. When the last bundles were removed, unbelievable numbers were seen, scurrying about in all directions.

There was a machine called a shredder that could be used to remove ears from corn bundles and shred the stocks and leaves so they could be eaten and digested more easily by cattle. My father found a used shredder and purchased it for fifty dollars. It had the appearance of a small threshing machine, with its feeder in front and blower behind, and was operated in much the same manner.

Not only was drilled corn put through this machine, but some of our checked corn as well. This gave us greater control on the amount of grain to be fed with the fodder, but there was substantially more work involved in the process. The corn had to be cut and shocked, and later a crew was necessary to bring the bundles in from the field if the shredder was to be operated efficiently. We did not have adequate manpower for this. On one occasion, additional help was hired, but this was too expensive to continue, and we did not have time during the fall to do extensive shredding without such help. As a result, our shredder did not receive as much use as Dad would have preferred.

'After the first frost, the corn plant rapidly died and the ears began losing their high moisture content. Corncribs, used to store ear corn, were constructed with spaces between the horizontal siding to permit free circulation of air so the corn could continue to dry; however, it was still necessary for the moisture content of the ears to be low enough to store in the crib. When such was the case, picking began. (Modern pickers pick and shell the corn in the field and the shelled corn is then put in a dryer until its moisture content is low enough to store in an enclosed bin.)

As previously noted, mechanical corn pickers had made their appearance; however, extensive handpicking was still in evidence. Many farmers continued to pick by hand exclusively, and use of the earlier model mechanical pickers, such as ours, did not eliminate this activity. A brief look at this labor-intensive task is in order.

The days at this time of the year were quite short and all daylight hours had to be used for picking. As a result, chores and other related activities were performed early enough so that we would be in the field with the wagons when the ears became visible. Triple-wagon boxes were used with three additional bank boards for the pickers to toss the ears against. The reins from the team were tied to the wagon, and they were trained to go forward or stop at the command of "giddap" and "whoa." Picking was done from the left side.

Corn husks and kernels are abrasive, and long sleeves and cotton gloves were a necessity. Dad also put old stockings over his arms. Double-thumbed, cotton gloves rapidly wore through, but were purchased by the dozen and turned over and used on the other side when one side had worn through.

Two different tools were available to facilitate hand picking— the hook and the pick. The hook consisted of a small, metal plate with a half-inch hook attached and riveted to leather straps that fastened on the palm of the right hand over the glove. The pick consisted of a piece of metal, shaped like a can opener used to punch triangle-shaped holes in metal cans. It was strapped to the fingers of the right hand. We used the hook, except for Mother, who used the pick when she assisted Dad in this task after Wilbur and I left home.

Pickers picked the two rows adjacent to the wagon, proceeding down the field and always looking ahead for the next ear to pick while giving verbal instructions to the team. They grasped the ear at the silk end with the left hand, tore the husk from the right side of the ear with the hook in the right hand, pulled the rest of the husk away from the ear with the left hand and snapped the ear off with one hand while holding the stem with the other. Thus the term "snapping corn" came to be used. The ear was tossed into the wagon. Each picker kept the location of the wagon's bank board in the corner of his eye so it was not necessary to look at the wagon when tossing the ear. This action soon became routine and was quickly and automatically performed.

While oats were shocked during the hottest time of the year, corn was picked during some of the coldest and most miserable weather. It was common for farmers to be picking corn between Thanksgiving and Christmas, and not unusual to see some in the field after the first of the new year. There was frost on the ears in the morning and gloves soon became soaking wet. Our hands then joined our feet in becoming numb from the cold. Strong wrist action was required to snap the ears and often wrists were sprained. Picking could not be stopped for such minor ailments, and even though substantial amounts of Sloans liniment and Ben Gay were used, sprained wrists usually remained sore throughout the picking season. Extensive salves were also used to control chapping, but this balm seemed to do little to ease the condition.

The goal of all corn pickers was to pick one hundred bushels a day, a goal that depended not only on the picker's ability, but also on the quality of the corn being picked. If many of the stocks contained small ears, called nubbins, or if a substantial number of ears were lying on the ground or attached to broken stocks, the volume of corn picked was drastically reduced. The yield of open pollinated corn seldom exceeded sixty bushels per acre and few pickers could pick a hundred bushels a day. When given a choice, professional pickers chose farmers with high-yield crops.

During the last few years we lived at Ledyard, our corn was

picked entirely by hand. Dad hired a professional to assist us and his only task was to pick corn and unload his own loads. He was given five cents a bushel and board and room. Dad furnished the team and wagon, but the picker had to take care of them. Since he had no chores other than taking care of his team, he would go to the field before we did, but often it was so dark he could make little headway before we arrived. He averaged about two loads of forty bushels each day.

Corn-picking contests were popular and were held at the county, state, and national level. Fields for these contests were carefully chosen and prepared. The contestants were engaged in picking for only a few hours, and as a result, their production was quite high. They were judged for the amount of corn picked and penalized for husk left on ears and the number of ears left in the field after picking. Dad and I attended a county contest held north of Lakota one year, but it was not an especially thrilling affair. I was too familiar with such activity to become excited.

During the first few years at Ledyard, we did not have an elevator and it was necessary to unload our wagons by using a scoop. The scoop board, which attached to the rear of the wagon in lieu of the end gates, pivoted down for unloading so that the scooper had a platform to stand on as he progressed into the wagon. Two different kinds of scoops were used: a tined scoop, made especially for ear corn, and a regular solid grain scoop. It was not an easy task, especially when the corn had to be lifted several feet into the air to the top of a nearly full crib. Corn pickers were given an extra cent per bushel when they had to unload their wagons with a scoop.

In 1931 Dad purchased a used elevator and, after some repairs, it was used to unload our grain. It hoisted the grain up a sloping chute by means of two parallel chains with slat links placed about one foot apart. The chute consisted of segments bolted together so its length could be changed by adding or removing segments. It was supported on a wood frame that had wheels so it could be moved about by a team of horses. The chute was raised and lowered between two wooden vertical supports by means of a cable hoist. The portion into which the grain was dumped rested on the ground and was hinged so that it could be put in a vertical position to permit wagons to pass.

Initially, the elevator was powered by a team attached to a boom and walking in circles around a turntable. Power was transferred to the elevator through rotating rods and universal joints, and these were also used to transfer power from the elevator to our U-shaped, steel-framed hoist that raised the front of our wagons a few feet to facilitate unloading.

The first wagon would be positioned with the front wheels directly under the hoist with the hoist cables attached to the front wheel hubs through the spokes; the team would be unhitched and placed on the turntable; the portion of the elevator behind the wagon was lowered, and the team began to power the machine while the operator opened the lower end gate. This end gate was hinged at the center and was gradually opened to control the number of ears falling into the elevator. As the rear of the wagon began to empty, the front was slowly rising, causing the grain to slide to the rear.

When the wagon was empty, the front of the wagon was lowered, that portion of the elevator behind the wagon was raised, and the empty wagon was manually rolled away from the hoist so that the next wagon could enter. The team on the second wagon then pulled its wagon into position and the process was repeated. It was not necessary to remove the team from the wagon when it was raised in the hoist.

Later, Dad purchased a used, single-cylinder, three-horsepower, air-cooled engine to power the elevator. It was mounted on wheels and was moved about with a team. A kit, containing clutch, shafts, and pulley, was purchased, and Wilbur made a clutch box, using heavy planks and rods. This eliminated the need for switching horses during this operation.

The elevator not only reduced the time and effort required to unload, but it also permitted corn to be stacked higher in our temporary snow fence corncribs. Although crude in operation, its use was much preferred to scooping.

While some hand picking was performed every year, the use of our mechanical picker continued at Ledyard during our first years there. The V-2 engine provided power for the mechanism until the cock in the oil pan was inadvertently opened. This time Dad could not stop the engine before excessive vibration and knocking broke the engine block. We mounted our Model T engine onto the picker, and it was used in this fashion until its retirement.

The need for hand picking when using the mechanical picker needs clarification. Corn stalks enter modern corn pickers directly from the front and the machine does not extend to the side beyond the rows being picked; therefore, they can enter an unpicked field and harvest it without knocking down unpicked corn. Such was not the case with our picker. It picked one row of corn on the left side of the machine while the picking paraphernalia, the horses, the main part of the machine, and the adjacent team and wagon extended to the right for four rows. These rows were trampled over, and unless previously picked, the ears would be knocked to the ground where the picker could not retrieve them later. These rows, on the entire perimeter of the field and intermittent strips in between, were picked by hand before the mechanical picker was used.

When the mechanical picker was in use, both wagons were taken to the field, using the picker horses on one of the wagons. When the first wagon was full, its team was transferred to the second. When both were full, picking ceased while the loads were taken to the corncrib to be unloaded. (This was also when the extensive lubrication tasks took place.) When operations proceeded normally, six wagon loads were picked daily.

Our corn-picking duties were not over when the mechanical picker was through. The weight of the more desirable large ears on open pollinated corn tended to overstress their supporting stems, breaking some in the process and permitting them to fall to the ground where the picker could not retrieve them. A few ears were also knocked to the ground by the picker fork before the rollers could grasp the stock. (One of the characteristics bred into hybrid corn was a more sturdy stock and stem. A more sturdy stem would, of course, have made hand picking more difficult.) Dad did not intend to abandon these ears, so the last corn-picking task involved gleaning the areas picked by the mechanical picker. This was generally done by two men, each taking three rows as they proceeded down the field, picking the ears up from the ground, husking them, and throwing them into an adjacent wagon.

Although much tedious and unpleasant hand picking was eliminated by the use of our machine, it is obvious that the operation was not an efficient one. As noted on page 33, improved two-row, tractor-powered pickers soon appeared and these machines reduced, and eventually eliminated, the need for hand picking. One brand of picker was mounted on the tractor—the forerunner of the self-propelled giants of today.

SOYBEANS

Although they became a major cash crop for us later at Manly, we did not grow soybeans at Ledyard. Small combines were coming into use for small grain and they were also used to harvest soybeans. This took place in the fall before corn picking began.

SUGAR BEETS

We never grew sugar beets but some farmers did, including Ed Donji, our neighbor to the south. Extensive manual labor was required to grow sugar beets and Ed used a Mexican family to assist him. They were housed in a small building in the field. The entire family, including small children, worked many hours in the field thinning and weeding the beets with a hoe. Later, the mature beets were topped, using a large knife.

MISCELLANEOUS FIELDWORK

Although breaking sod was no longer a common task, Dad broke our few acres of original prairie in 1933. He broke sod by taking one bottom off the three-bottom tractor plow and pulling it with the Hart Parr. The tractor was in its declining years and did not have the power it once had, so even though only two bottoms were being used, much of the work had to be done in low gear.

Centuries of prairie grass roots were embedded in this soil and as the plow slowly moved down the field, two giant strips of black soil were left in its wake. The result was a field of neatly laid, unbroken strips of sod, quietly awaiting a new fate.

It was necessary to disk this area using horses and make it responsive to the growing of new and different plants. The wheels of this implement found it difficult to penetrate the leatherlike sod, even though stones were strapped on its top for additional weight. The newly tilled soil showed its disdain for this course of action by subjecting the implement and rider to exceptionally large bumps and jerks, making this task unusually unpleasant.

I understand that many pioneers used flax for their first crop on newly broken prairie because they believed that it was more efficient than other crops in breaking sod. We did not grow flax so our first crop was corn. Great difficulty was experienced in the planting and cultivation the first year and the number of corn plants reaching maturity was not great. The unnourished prairie grass roots soon died and the following year the rich soil was actively participating in its new role of being some of the best in the world for the growing of nitrogen-demanding corn.

A task no longer required, but one we performed, was the removal of large rocks from the fields. On their departure, the glaciers had left these calling cards in the soil, and although most had been extracted from our cultivated areas, a few remained, including those in our newly broken prairie. When partially exposed, we could work around them, but when buried just below the ground, they were a menace. On two occasions, I was nearly thrown from a plow when it struck these unseen obstacles, and breaking a plow share was a distinct possibility. Some tractor plows, including the two-bottom plow we used later on the Fordson, had an automatic release built into the pulling tongue that would detach the implement from the tractor when an unusually large impact was encountered. This offered some protection, but obviously, the rock's removal was preferred.

Those that could be dug up and rolled onto the stoneboat were soon dispatched to the rock pile adjacent to the barn, but the larger ones had to be broken up into manageable pieces first, which required dynamite. Any adult could purchase dynamite from local stores and Dad always had a small quantity of 40 percent strength on hand, with a roll of fuse and some caps. The first charge was directly on top. He estimated how many sticks would be required, cut a sufficient length of fuse from the roll, and pushed one end into the open end of a cap; one of the sticks of dynamite was opened at one end, a small amount of material removed, and the cap with fuse inserted. Everything was covered with mud before we lit the fuse and strolled a sufficient distance away to observe. If near the road, I was placed to stop traffic that might come by. After the rock had been broken, a second charge was placed underneath the pieces to blow them out of the ground so they could be easily placed on a stoneboat.

TRACTORS

The availability of low-cost, distillate fuels and the introduction of power takeoffs just before the 1920s resulted in a rapid increase in the use of tractors for fieldwork. This technological advance quickly produced changes, a few of which will be noted.

When first introduced, many power takeoff shafts and universal joints had insufficient shielding, and the ability to operate the mechanism while the machine was at rest permitted close inspection of these and other rapidly moving parts. The smooth shafts appeared incapable of grasping a pant leg or shirt sleeve and the removal of shields to make these inspections easier was not unknown. Although they appeared innocent, the ability of these shafts to grasp clothing was phenomenal, and when they did, in less time than it takes to blink an eye, the amazing tensile strength of the garments crushed leg and arm bones as they coiled about the shafts, not infrequently detaching a limb in the process. Needless to say, the safety record of machinery operators was not an impressive one until they acquired sufficient respect for power machinery.

The use of power takeoffs eliminated the need for lugged bull wheels, but lugs were still needed on the rear wheels of tractors. Their use in the field was not uncomfortable, but on hard-surfaced roads, the bumpy response dictated the need for maintaining a very slow speed. They were also destructive when used on paved roads, and as these roads made their appearance, signs were posted, stating that no lugged vehicles were permitted to travel on them.

The tractors produced before and in the early 1920s were designed primarily for plowing or belt work and were either a two- or three-bottom size, with horsepower noted as 10–20 or 15–30. (The first number was the drawbar power, the second was the horsepower available from the pulley when using a belt.) However, the introduction of International Harvester's Farmall and other row crop-type tractors during this decade permitted their use with cultivators, eliminating the need to keep horses for this fieldwork. Their tricycle wheel arrangement permitted the front wheel(s) to go between two rows while the back wheels were spaced far enough apart, or were made adjustable like the John Deere models A and B, to straddle two rows and were large enough in diameter for the axle to pass over knee-high corn. Although this configuration provided less stability from the standpoint of overturning, the machine proved to be popular and remained in use until herbicides and pesticides made the use of cultivators unnecessary.

The introduction of rubber tires on tractors in the 1930s proved to be the last blow to the use of the draft horse. Rubber tires made the use of tractors more comfortable and versatile under all conditions, especially for rapid towing. Not only could they be used on all road surfaces, but they could also be used at higher speeds, making them an ideal replacement for horses when taking farm commodities to market in wagons. This, of course, led to the greater use of tires on the implements being towed.

The physical effort required to raise and lower gangs of cultivator shovels at each end of the field and to operate other accessories soon led to the development of hydraulic controls, and higher speeds dictated the need for better steering mechanisms. The electrical systems quickly included starters, and tractor operation became as easy and comfortable as a car.

After our Hart Parr could no longer be used for fieldwork, Dad wanted to purchase a new machine, but reality dictated the lowering of his sights. On one occasion, he mentioned the possibility of getting a used Model D John Deere, but even this modest goal was to elude him. There was to be no replacement for the Hart Parr until 1936, and it proved to be less than ideal.

Ed Donji had a Fordson tractor, whose loud groaning sound from its worm gear drive was familiar to everyone in the neighborhood. The fact that Ed had to frequently release the clutch and permit the engine to catch its breath and regain its normal operation RPMs was evidence that it had obviously lost some of its power. When the clutch was reengaged, the moaning returned, gradually decreasing in pitch as the tractor slowed down to the point where Ed would have to repeat the process. Ed had experienced some difficulty with this machine and during the summer of 1936 it broke down in his field adjacent to our farm. He walked over to where Dad was working and said he was getting rid of the machine; if Dad would remove it from his field, it was his for ten dollars. Dad gave him the money and we had ourselves a "new" tractor.

It could not be towed until the worm gear was removed. A team brought the machine to our farmyard, where extensive internal operations were performed. A used, two-bottom plow was purchased and the tractor's performance was observed. It was not a powerful machine, but could handle the two, fourteen-inch bottoms on most ground. Because every penny was needed to make our move to Manly and fuel was in short supply, testing was brief and further use of this machine was delayed until 1937. At Manly, this tractor was to provide me with countless experiences, not the least of which involved mechanical repair.

Hooves and Feathers

The diversified farm of the early 1900s had several kinds of domestic animals: horses, cattle, hogs, and chickens being the most prominent. Sheep were not raised extensively in our community and mutton was a dish I never tasted until I left home. We raised turkeys one year at Lakota but never raised ducks, geese, or guinea hens.

Like most farmers, we did our own castrating and dehorning and performed other minor operations on our animals when necessary. As economic conditions deteriorated after the 1929 stock market crash, we could not afford the services of a veterinarian, even for the more serious operations, and in many cases these too were performed by us. I recall a veterinarian being called only once in the eight years we lived at Ledyard. This was to save a cow that had been in labor many hours, and even with Dad's help, was unable to dislodge the dead calf. Consequently, farm boys received extensive on-the-job-training in these activities.

HORSES

Horses are not the most intelligent animal, but they are attractive, usually have good personalities (except for stallions), and are easily trained to be faithful servants. These factors, combined with their large size, made them ideal beasts of burden, a role they continued to play into the 1930s. The car had then replaced horse-drawn vehicles for personal transportation, and the introduction of better and more versatile tractors resulted in their disappearance in the field. However, the depression was to dampen, and in some cases temporarily reverse, this movement. My first few years of fieldwork were to take place using horse power exclusively. Mules—a sterile cross between a male donkey and female horse—were also in evidence and were considered by some to be more hardy and better at pulling heavy loads than the horse. But they had a reputation of being more stubborn and most farmers, like Dad, used horses exclusively.

When we moved to Ledyard, we had seven horses, permitting the use of five in the field and one team for miscellaneous tasks. I don't know their breed, but I suspect that they were a combination of several of the more common ones used for draft horses. Many farmers raised their own, using the services of available community stallions, and I recall Dad doing so on one occasion. The resulting colt did not survive and Dad returned to his practice of purchasing horses as required.

The males were transformed into geldings and when all young horses were old enough for pulling tasks, they were broken to the plow by placing them in a harness between two "old timers." With the driver at the rear, going forward was the only sensible course of action. Heavy pulling soon dampened their enthusiasm for sprinting or other unnecessary physical activity, and they quickly adapted to a subservient role.

Horse traders were in generous supply but the term had a somewhat negative connotation similar to that now occasionally implied in the expression "used car salesman." Great care was necessary in buying a horse. Like a car, a horse's physical appearance could be inspected and appear perfectly normal, but qualities and traits not visible could prove to be just as important. On one occasion, my father purchased a horse that viciously kicked every time the belly band on the harness was tightened; he had to be sold. Then on another occasion, he purchased Maude, of whom more will be said later.

All animals, except those kept in the pasture, had to be taken care of daily, but none more so than the horse. Horse operators fed and watered their horses before taking care of their own needs, and when heavy pulling was involved, oats were an important part of their diet. (Thus, the expression "oats burner.")

Horses had to be shod when extensively used on gravel or hard-surfaced roads, and blacksmiths performed this task for those who did not do their own. Horses that were used exclusively on the farm, such as ours, did not require this accessory, but their hoofs needed trimming periodically. Although this is not painful, such activity is not to the horse's liking, which meant that working on the horse's major defense weapon called for caution. A rope loop, attached to the end of a small stick, was twisted around the horse's nose because for some unexplained reason, this calmed the horse down. One of us held the horse in this fashion, while Dad used a chisel and hammer to trim the excess material from the hoof, which had generally split as it had spread.

Because teams were used for many different tasks, at least one was always kept available in the barn. The other horses, if not immediately needed for fieldwork, were put out to pasture in the summer. However, getting them back in the barn when needed was not always an easy task. They valued their freedom and they frequently resisted when we attempted to steal it. A battle usually developed between man and beast, with the beast very much in control. Horses that were docile and friendly when in the barn could not be approached closely when in the pasture; it was not because of their fear of physical harm but rather their desire to evade the strenuous work they knew awaited them that made them difficult at these times.

Each team had its own assigned stall and each horse its assigned place in that stall. There was a manger in front of each stall for feeding hay and an individual grain box for each horse. Halters were used to keep them in their assigned place and each horse had its own harness that hung on a wooden peg on the back wall.

Serious injuries, such as getting their hooves tangled in barbed wire, were occasionally encountered, but the most common physical problem was collar sores. The fit of a horse's collar was very important and the hide at the point of contact between horse and collar needed a little time to adjust and toughen up— time that was frequently not available at the beginning of fieldwork in the spring. It was at this point that sores developed and since field operations could not cease, healing became difficult. Home remedies consisted of the application of salves, kerosene, or motor oils.

Harnesses consisted of many parts including a hame, which fit firmly in a groove on the collar, the trace or pulling straps that were attached to the hame, and a breeching strap around the rear of the horse for use in backing up. A tongue was required on the vehicle for backing up and a neck yoke, which attached to the hame, exerting the backward thrust to the tongue. Horses were controlled by the bits in their bridles; bits were available in several types, from simple, one-piece affairs for those easily controlled to the more complicated ones that consisted of several metal parts fitted together for those requiring greater restraint. Side blinders were part of the bridles and were a simple piece of leather placed next to the eyes so that the horse could not see to the side. A nose guard was provided with each bridle and was used when the horses were working in fields where they could eat and damage the crop, such as when cultivating knee-high corn; they consisted of a simple screen or leather basket that was placed over the nose and mouth. Fly nets were used during fly time to reduce the disturbing influence of these blood suckers. (The horse fly, an unusually large member of this family, was particularly vicious when in pursuit of a meal.)

Harnesses required periodic maintenance, including oiling, and this was generally a rainy or winter day task. As we progressed into the depression, their repair became more frequent and extensive. Leather and metal parts from old discarded harnesses had to be used.

In 1935 our repairs ceased to provide the degree of integrity needed for our first team and Dad was forced to purchase a new set. The catalogs contained several pages of harnesses for sale, from the simple to the highly decorative; it was not an expensive or highly decorative one that we received in the mail. The parts had to be assembled and individually fitted to each horse, and we joined the threshing crew without fear of a possible embarrassing breakdown.

When working with animals many hours each day, individual traits become obvious and personalities begin to stand out. Attachment to some animals more so than others soon became apparent, which was the case with me. Several of our horses come to mind.

Bess was a hard worker; she and Fanny were our first team, the one used for miscellaneous tasks about the farm. She was pleasant to work with and was generally cooperative, but she had one trait that occasionally gave us trouble; when she encountered a load she could not pull with the initial effort, she gave up and refused to try again. This trait was acquired after Wilbur and I attempted to have the team pull a load from our gravel pit that was too heavy.

We were in the pit with a single box on the wagon and had just completed filling it. When we were attempting to leave, Bess and Fanny strained at their harnesses but the wagon refused to budge. After a few attempts, Bess refused to try again and Wilbur and I had to virtually empty the box before Fanny could move the wagon by herself. Once the wagon moved, Bess joined in, but after this incident whatever she was pulling had to move on the first try or she refused further participation.

Bess had one other trait that needed watching—one acquired as a result of being the recipient of shotgun pellets as noted on page 84. Although the pellets did little damage physically, such was not the case mentally. Thereafter, the sight of any gun caused her to react in a violent manner. Even pitchforks made her nervous and she could not tolerate anyone standing immediately in front of her manger for any length of time.

Dick was a gelding and a workaholic. It made no difference where he was or what he was pulling, he gave his all and continued to do so all day. I recall one occasion where this trait gave me some trouble.

We were disking plowed ground, a task requiring heavy pulling with the horses walking on soft ground, and as usual, Dick went all out. Eveners were attached so that all horses had to pull the same amount to keep them even, but the chains connecting the harness to the single tree could be connected long or short, and I connected Dick's near the end so that he would project in front of the other horses. I had hoped that this would discourage him from setting an excessively fast pace. The horses were given periodic rests, but I could not hold Dick back and he soon became literally wet with sweat. Late in the afternoon, he stumbled and fell to the ground, unable to get up. Substantial effort was necessary on my part to get him on his feet again, and our fieldwork was terminated for the day.

He survived and although we exercised greater care in using him, he never ceased being a workaholic. We were not without feelings in these matters; we had a great deal of empathy for animals such as Dick, but unfortunately, timely completion of our fieldwork was necessary for our survival.

Maude had the appearance of a good work horse when Dad purchased her; she was muscular, had good teeth and no apparent defects. She was brought home, put on the disk with four other horses, and we proceeded down the field.

However, it was soon apparent that she was extremely lazy.

She refused to pull and the single tree to which she was attached rode unceremoniously back against the disk. I fastened her harness short so that she lagged behind the others when pulling, hoping this would encourage her to do more, but this was not to be. I spent much of my time picking up clods of dirt and throwing them at her, but this was obviously no solution. When I returned to the field in the afternoon, I carried a small wood stick, but it had little effect on Maude's tough hide. Other means were obviously required and my BB gun came to mind.

My lever action BB gun was not a lethal weapon; on several occasions, a portion of my anatomy had been a target and my thin clothes prevented the BB from doing any real damage. However, a target was subject to a strong sting. The next day, it was hanging from one of the control levers as we started down the field.

Although the BB did not leave a wound and there was never any evidence of impact, the sting was something Maude was not accustomed to and a spurt of pulling resulted from each shot. Soon the metallic sound the gun made as it was removed from its wire hanger was sufficient to encourage a burst of activity, but periodic shots were still necessary when she began to assume I was only bluffing. Because she was never sure when I was bluffing, she began to look back to keep an eye on me. Her blinders on her bridle forced her to turn her head 180 degrees and look straight back. She was soon spending every day, all day, walking forward while looking straight back. She was, indeed, unique. I have been unable to find in the many annals of horse lore any records of such a horse, and the effect of her actions on me were not limited to the field. When sleeping during the next several weeks, my right arm would involuntarily reach out periodically to grab an imaginary BB gun, not unlike the actions of a gambler operating a one-armed bandit in Las Vegas.

There were those who loved working with horses, but I was not one of them. Operators of horse-drawn farm machinery had front row seats where they observed only that end of the horse frequently mentioned in a derogatory manner, and the horses were not positioned in tandem but were lined up side by side so that a close-up view of all the horses was unavoidable. In this position, determined by trial and error over a substantial period of time, operators were in the direct line of fire of all discharged solids, liquids, and gases, usually disposed of in enormous quantities. The resulting environment was such that we found tractors without mufflers and spewing obnoxious exhaust gases a virtual paradise by comparison. We all have pleasant visions when describing the unique physical features and activities of favorite pets, but when any portion of the body held in low esteem predominates such visions, it does not intensify the bond that supposedly exists between man and beast.

CATTLE

Cattle provided us with butterfat and beef—the cream was a small but continuous source of income and the steers were an annual source of assistance in making the mortgage or rent payments. There were breeds that were best for each purpose. For example, guernseys or holsteins produced good butterfat and angus was the best beef. However, keeping two breeds was not practical and Dad joined the majority of farmers in using short horns for both purposes. The breed was not the best, or worst, of either, but a good compromise for both.

Although our cattle, except for the bull, were not aggressive, temperaments differed and some were more pleasant to work with than others. Each was unique but, unlike our horses, none had a name. Our herd was not large, and since personal contact was made with the cows twice a day, they were observed especially closely. Some had udders of gigantic proportions that nearly touched the ground and produced large quantities of milk, while others had delicate and petite mammary features that were less productive but more aesthetic.

It is perhaps fitting that those who differed most from the norm are the ones we remember. One such cow stands out. Shortly after becoming fresh, she began entering the barn for milking with an empty udder. There were no calves in the pasture to suckle her and she was the only cow in this condition. We began observing her in the pasture to determine the cause. Although we suspected that she was suckling herself, we had never heard of a cow doing so and could not see how it could be accomplished. It soon became apparent that, although difficult to do, it could and, in this case, was being done. She did so by lying on the ground and turning her body and head sharply around where she could just reach her teats with her mouth. In this strained and uncomfortable position, she managed to suckle for short periods of time, and after repeated attempts, emptied her udder. It was apparent that we had a problem.

She was a good milk producer, so our first thought was to construct some device to prevent her from continuing this practice. An iron chastity device that covered her udder was considered, but this would be difficult to attach and could very well inhibit milk production. Because she could barely reach her teats with her mouth, it appeared that a stiff, high collar would suffice to prevent her from reaching them. This was the course of action taken. A collar, consisting of a number of boards approximately sixteen inches long and fastened together with leather straps, was constructed and attached around her neck. We then observed her in the pasture.

Although the collar hindered it did not entirely prevent her from suckling herself. However, greater time and effort was spent in the pursuit. Another collar slightly longer was tried and because she spent a substantial part of the day in this activity, she eventually succeeded as she had before. It was obvious that an even longer collar would adversely affect her grazing activity, so no further consideration was given to this course of action. Keeping her in the barn night and day indefinitely was not a feasible solution, so Dad took the only course of action he could—he sold her to the slaughter house.

The county periodically tested all milk cows to prevent the spread of tuberculosis, and when a cow tested positive, it was destroyed and the farmer reimbursed. On one occasion, one of our cows had a positive test and was destroyed. Naturally, it was our best milk producer.

Artificial insemination was not yet in use and a bull was a necessity for the raising of cattle. Bulls had to be replaced periodically to prevent inbreeding, and farmers frequently exchanged or borrowed each other's bulls. A few farmers kept their bull tethered in the barn with a ring through its nose, letting it have contact with the cows for breeding purposes only. However, most, including Dad, let their bulls run with the cows.

A bull has the tendency to become a very aggressive animal when a cow that is his romantic attachment is temporarily removed from his presence. When the cows were put in the barn for milking, great care was necessary and the presence of our dog was advised.

Newborn calves were immediately removed from the mother's presence and kept in a separate pen in the barn. This was done to prevent the calf from drinking more milk than necessary and to bring the cow up to maximum milk production by completely emptying her udder twice a day. Because the mothers were naturally protective of their young, this had to be done with care. When born in the pasture, the stoneboat was used to bring the calf to the barn with the mother in close attendance, making sure that no other animals approached her calf.

Feeding a newborn calf was not an easy task. The calf's natural inclination is to suckle its mother's teats and periodically butt the mother's udder, apparently an inducement for the mother to release milk. Weaning required an alternate milk source, but when a calf's head was forced into a bucket with its mouth and nose below the surface of the milk, it did not know what to do. A finger was generally used to imitate a teat, and with the milk that entered its nose when breathing, it soon tasted the milk and began sucking. At the same time that the calf's head was held in the bucket, the bucket had to be firmly held to prevent the periodic butting from spilling the milk. The sight of milk spurting from the calf's nose as its head was periodically raised, the milk spilling against our trousers from frequent butting, and the gymnastics necessary for us to remain on our feet, presented a scene of utter chaos, which it usually proved to be.

Calves were kept in the barn until they were old enough to graze and do without milk. When old enough, they were put in the pasture with the other cattle. Their first outdoor exposure confused them. Their world had been the four solid walls of the barn where they could stand up and walk but not run, like the wide open spaces of the pasture induced them to do. A few short attempts at running quickly led to greater confidence and then they began running at breakneck speed with tails straight up in the air. We called this high tailing. Because they did not know what a fence was and did not recognize it as a barrier, they invariably ended up tangled in barbed wire. This sobering introduction to fences appeared to hurt them, and gashes in their hide were common, but I recall no serious injuries from this activity. One such experience was generally sufficient to make them respect fences, and future high tailing was restricted to areas somewhat distant from fences.

Although our breed was called short horn, they still grew horns; the removal of the horns was necessary to prevent the cattle from injuring each other and to permit easy insertion of the cows' heads into stanchions. The horns began their growth when the calves were quite young and as soon as they protruded a few inches from the skull, they were removed. This was done by placing a rope around the neck of the calf, pulling it through a stanchion in the barn, tensioning the rope with a block and tackle wire stretcher sufficient to limit side-to-side head movement, and using a dehorning saw, one similar to a butcher's saw, to cut the horn off flush with the skull. Blood could be seen spurting several feet as the heart beat and flour was placed over the wound to encourage coagulation. Horns had to be cut off close to the skull or they would grow back and require a repeat operation.

Male calves were not permitted to maintain their manhood unless they were to be used for breeding, and since few were required for this purpose, most were castrated and became steers. Steers were considered necessary because they could be fattened more quickly than bulls who used energy in romantic pursuits, and steers' tender flesh was much preferred over the baloney-type meat obtained from bulls. Castration was performed when the animals were quite young and easy to control and when the traumatic effects would be less. I held the animal down while Dad, using a special, finely honed pocketknife, used only for this purpose, proceeded to cut through the sack, grab the testicles, and sever the attaching cords. This was done without an anesthetic and the reaction of the calf was predictable.

We did not consume the testicles. It was not until some years later that I became aware that mountain oysters, lamb fries, and such were not only edible but were considered delicacies by some. My one experience with eating them leads me to believe that if properly prepared, they are tender and delicious, but their origin and purpose has instilled within me a bias against such consumption, a bias I find difficult to overcome.

Under certain grazing conditions cattle can develop a flatulent digestive disturbance marked by abdominal bloating. If the condition becomes severe enough it subjects the animal to intense pain and can result in death if the gas is not released. The only means of releasing the gas is by sticking the animal with a stiletto in just the right location, penetrating the hide and gas pocket and permitting the release of the gas. The sticking must be done in the proper manner and in the right location, and if properly performed, saves the animal from a very painful death. The eating habits of these animals can be controlled to minimize this problem and we had no such difficulty at Ledyard. Although

I was not on the scene to observe the procedure, I do recall one such instance at Lakota, when Dad saved an animal by sticking it.

Cows were frequently given grain such as ground oats or corn to increase milk production, and during the time of the year when cattle could not graze, they had to be fed hay. Shelling a sufficient amount of corn in the hand sheller to feed all our animals was too great a task, so the entire ear was ground. (We had our own grinder and ground our own, using the Hart Parr.) Although the cob had little nutritive value, it no doubt contributed to a feeling of contentment due to its filling quality, and the cattle seemed to like the taste of the combination. Later at Manly, the cows were fed silage.

Several weeks before steers were sent to market, they were separated from the other cattle and put in a separate feed lot to be finished. Here they were given all the grain they could eat and exercise was discouraged. (Feed supplements and hormones, antibiotics, and such were not yet in use.) They remained in the feed lot until they had gained sufficient weight and the market seemed right. When the time for selling approached, Dad monitored the market quotations (by radio, if possible) and when all factors were favorable or the need for mortgage or rent money dictated the time of sale, final preparations were made.

During the hours just before the steers were loaded onto the trucks, they were encouraged not only to eat as much as they could but to drink as much water as possible. Although Dad never did, some farmers used liberal amounts of salt to encourage drinking. When they had reached their full capacity, they were loaded and taken to the buyers.

Farmers could sell their animals directly to the packing plant or to local buyers. At Ledyard, the time, effort, and cost of trucking to a distant packing plant usually convinced farmers to sell locally. I recall one occasion when Dad hired a truck to take a load of steers directly to the packing plant. Upon his return, he said he had received just enough more money to pay the trucker. Later when we lived at Manly, the Albert Lea, Minnesota, and Mason City, Iowa, packing plants were close by and we generally took our animals directly to the packing plant. When trucked a substantial distance, buyers considered the shrinkage caused from eliminating wastes that took place during transit before they quoted prices. Animals could be sold for an agreed lump sum or by the pound, based on live weight. Dad figured that buyers, either local or at the packing plant, were professionals and could better estimate the weight of the animals than he could, so he always sold his animals by the pound.

HOGS

Hogs were an important source of income for most farmers and were occasionally referred to as mortgage raisers. Poland Chinas and Chester Whites were the most popular breeds. Although the purity of the blood line left much to be desired, we had Chester Whites. The frequent exchange of boars with other farmers resulted in a breed of dubious purity. Unlike today's hogs that have been designed to produce lean meat, ours were encouraged to become fat and produce large amounts of lard used for cooking.

The hog's reputation is not a good one, due in part to negative views concerning its personal habits. Their food preferences, anything from dead animals to choice morsels of manure, aggressive and "hoggish" eating manners, and their personal hygiene (wallowing in mud holes) were atrocious. However, they were one of the most intelligent animals on the farm. They could not be made into beasts of burden, but they learned how to go through poorly constructed fences, and they were difficult to control. However, hogs had at least one redeeming feature—when penned up, they were the only animal that chose a corner of the pen for a bathroom where all eliminated their waste, keeping the rest of the pen relatively clean and comfortable.

Their ability to learn and remember how to go through or root under fences was particularly vexing. Animals do not normally seek openings in or under fences unless they had some previous experience, but the condition of our fences permitted an occasional accidental escape and a hog always remembered how it could be repeated. They also used their snouts for rooting under fences to make their own escape route. Once these activities were learned, they were never forgotten and even rings in their noses and a good hog-tight fence would not assure a future free from escape. When hogs escaped from the yard, they pretended to be ignorant of how to get back in and they were stubborn, even when driven to an open gate. Sometimes we had to rely on Shep, who soon convinced them that going back into the yard was better than having their ears repeated perforated by canines in a less than soothing manner.

Since we had limited facilities to house our hogs, the arrival of piglets was arranged to escape severe winter weather. The boars ran freely with the sows and the piglets appeared three months, three weeks, and three days after breeding. A sow, lying contentedly on her side and grunting a periodic message that all is well while a line of piglets attack her nipples with gusto, is a peaceful, pleasant scene, but one that can be misleading. A sow is very protective of her young, and should a stranger enter her pen, she will attack without warning. Only Dad could enter our pens under such conditions, and if a piglet squealed while he was in the pen, even he was threatened.

When a mammary appendage ceased to provide a sufficient flow of milk, piglets made an attempt to detach a neighbor from his source, and fights ensued. These fights appeared to be vicious but the size of the piglets prevented serious injury. Unfortunately, there was always at least one runt who had difficulty maintaining his position and ended up sucking a dry one. This animal would frequently starve and die unless removed and fed separately.

The piglets were weaned and separated from their mothers as soon as they could eat and drink on their own. They were placed together in one large pen where the various litters fought each other until all were acquainted. Ultimately, fighting was restricted to occasional, personal differences and to the feed trough.

Soon after weaning, the sperm-producing organs on the males were large enough to be grasped and surgically removed, converting these males to barrows. One such experience comes to mind. The boar we had used had passed on an inherited tendency of rupturing when castrated, a fact not apparent until we began this operation on his offspring, and great care was necessary to prevent this from happening. Some sewing was required after removal of the organs, but one case of rupturing took place after the animal was back in the pen with the others. We were not aware of this until the other animals had pulled out and extensively chewed approximately twelve inches of intestine. The intestine was still intact so Dad attempted corrective surgery. An antiseptic was applied, the intestine was pushed carefully back into the abdominal cavity, and Dad was carefully sewing up the opening when the animal made a sudden tremendous effort to escape, using his abdominal muscles in the process. A portion of the intestine was forced back out through the smaller opening and a one-inch slit appeared in the intestine where it had been chewed. Dad sewed it up, but was not sure that it was tight enough to prevent future material from seeping out. He asked my opinion and together we decided to not subject it to more pain. This piglet became the exception to the rule that no hog was butchered before its time.

Hogs did not limit their rooting activity to making escape routes under fences. When in pastures, they used their snouts to root out grubs, worms, and other delicacies. Because this destroyed the pasture plants, we ringed them to discourage rooting activity of any kind. Hog rings were elliptical in shape with one side open and the ends tapered to an edge. The ring was placed in a hog ringer, a pliers-shaped tool, that held the ring while the operator placed the open end of the ring over the rim of the hog's snout. When properly positioned, the tool handles were quickly closed, forcing the two ends of the ring to penetrate the nose and come together to form a ring embedded in the rim of the snout. Several rings were generally placed in the nose of each hog. This did not entirely eliminate rooting, but drastically reduced it.

Hog cholera, a highly contagious and fatal hog disease, occasionally made its appearance and farmers were advised to vaccinate their animals against it. This required the services of a veterinarian and our financial circumstances convinced Dad that he should gamble and not do so. Fortunately, his gamble paid off and this grim reaper never made its appearance on our farm.

Corn and oats were our main hog feed. Although we did not carefully measure our feed, we were aware of the relative merits of selling corn by the bushel or on the hoof, depending on the corn/hog ratio and their relative prices. Such decisions obviously had to be made early, but in any case, we always had plenty of hogs to feed. Feed supplements were not used except for tankage, and this only as finances permitted. On a few occasions, there was a large animal carcass that the hogs were permitted to eat, which they would rapidly do, leaving only the large bones and hair. Small pigs found corn kernels difficult to remove from the ear and difficult to chew because of the flinty hardness of the kernels. For them, the corn had to be shelled and ground, or soaked oats were used as a substitute. Oats were placed in a barrel with water or skim milk for a day or until they had absorbed sufficient liquid and swelled to a substantially greater volume. The soggy result was a favorite of the small pigs. The soaked oats, swill from the house, and skim milk from the separator constituted the major portion of their diet.

When they became large enough to remove and chew kernels from the cob, ear corn was fed to them on the ground. We had a self-feeder which dispensed feed other than ear corn, but it was seldom used because the amount being fed could not be controlled and much of the feed would end up on the ground. The mixing of grain kernels and soil did not seem to disturb them; they were quite adept at removing food items from the soil. However, when plenty of feed was available, they made no attempt to recover that which fell on the ground.

When ready to be sold, our hogs were transported to market in our trailer, a few at a time, with the usual feeding and drinking binge preceding the trip.

CHICKENS

The production of eggs was the primary purpose for having chickens because egg money was the other source of income for daily living expenses. The folks always preferred leghorns, a somewhat smaller breed than some others and not as good at producing meat, but good layers for the amount of feed consumed. As previously noted, our incubator had been disposed of when we left the Lakota farm. Mother raised all our chicks by using setting or brooder hens the first few years at Ledyard. They were raised in the spring when the weather was mild and hens were getting into the brooding mood. Roosters were not necessary for merely producing eggs; they were, in fact, undesirable because fertilized eggs could spoil faster than unfertilized ones. However, they were necessary when using eggs to produce chicks. The brooding hens sat on their eggs the necessary three weeks, leaving their nest only for short periods of time to perform necessary life-sustaining activities. They were very protective of their eggs; any attempt to remove them resulted in vicious pecking.

After the chicks were hatched, the hens roamed with their broods, feeding on the ground corn that Mother cast in the farmyard. The chicks soon learned to scratch, looking for additional natural food. The mother hen provided as much defense as she could against intruders, but it often proved to be insufficient. It was at this age, when the chicks were small, that they were most tempting to cats. They also had to look out for other animals of prey, such as hawks. When raised in a brooder house, they were not permitted outside until they were a little older, and then they were fenced in and carefully watched.

When wet, small chicks quickly become chilled and would die if not immediately dried and warmed. The mothers sought protection for them when it rained, but if none was available, they sat on the chicks to keep them dry and warm. As soon as the sun began to set in the evening, they headed for the brooder house or other protective shelter.

It should be noted that the maternal instincts of our hens did not disappear when we began purchasing chicks from a hatchery. We had to discourage hens in their pursuit of this activity. Usually, we placed them in a chicken crate where they were given limited food and water and were unable to make a nest and be alone. Occasionally, a particularly stubborn hen had to be immersed in water a few times to dampen her desire to become a mother. There were a few occasions where a brooding hen made her nest, unknown to us, in a hidden place among the junk in our grove, and when her eggs were hatched, she would surprise us with her brood, which was generally few in number.

Hatching our own eggs was a tedious, time-consuming task, so after a few years Dad built a small separate brooder house and we began purchasing two to three hundred day-old chicks that were delivered by the mail carrier in cardboard boxes. Air holes were provided for breathing, and because a newborn chick can live a day or two without food or water, the mortality rate was low. They could be purchased mixed, about 50 percent males and females, or sexed, either males or females, and we purchased females only, even though they were the most expensive. The error in selection was about 5 percent, so we always had a few roosters to use as fryers.

The brooder house had to be kept at a constant warm temperature or the chicks would crowd together for warmth, and this bunching would invariably cause the death of many because of suffocation. Heating stoves could be purchased for brooder houses, but we used a portable kerosene stove. Its heat output could be adjusted but it did not have a thermostat, so it was necessary to check the temperature in the brooder house several times a day. Going to the brooder house at night was not an unusual experience for Mother or Dad.

Small chicks were highly susceptible to certain diseases, so they were carefully watched and any sickly ones were quickly removed. They tended to be cannibalistic and if for some reason a chick had an open wound, it had to be quickly removed or the others would peck it to death. Their feed consisted of finely ground corn or oats placed in small feeders or pans. They grew rapidly and were soon permitted out of the small fenced area near the brooder house. When they approached adulthood, they were put in the chicken house with the older birds.

Our roosters were too few in number to sell and were not caponized. They ran with the hens and because the male/female ratio was highly in their favor, each became a cock of the walk. When approximately two pounds in weight, they were considered fryers and eligible for the chopping block. After being caught by the dog, they were decapitated using a hatchet or knife.

Adult chickens were fed whole oats as well as coarsely ground corn. They preferred oats that were hulled, but we had no huller and taking oats to town for this process was an expense we did not assume. They require fine sand or other gritty material to grind up hard food particles in their gizzard, and the hens also needed sufficient calcium to form their egg shells. We purchased oyster shells by the sack to provide calcium and to supplement the normal gritty material they found in the soil.

Egg production varied throughout the year, depending on the weather and the number of laying hens. It was at a peak during the summer when we took thirty to forty-five dozen eggs to town three times a week. Each egg was inspected for cracks and dirt before being placed in the crate. Mother kept the cracked eggs for our consumption, and the dirty ones were cleaned with a damp cloth. They were candled at the grocery store where we did our trading. Apparently candles were originally used, but our candling was performed in a dark room where each egg was placed directly in front of a light bulb so that its contents could be viewed. Fertilized eggs that would develop rapidly in warm weather and spoiled or rotten eggs were removed. Mother took pride in having good eggs, so we got them to market fast and had few rejects. After candling, we received credit on our account for the good eggs. Although the price varied, the lowest amount we received was eight cents a dozen.

As fall approached, a certain number of our chickens heeded the call of the wild and roosted in our trees at night. They could not survive in this environment during the winter so it was necessary to catch and pen them up in the chicken house several days until they considered it suitable for their home. They were captured at night, using a hook that resembled a shepherd's crook. If carefully used, they could be caught by their legs without hurting them.

Not all hens were good layers and to maintain an efficient operation, it was necessary to remove the non- or poor-laying hens. This was done by culling, which is based on the belief that laying hens have larger egg-laying orifices than nonlayers. From this line of reasoning, it was assumed that the size of the orifice was directly proportional to the number of eggs laid. Therefore, the orifice of each hen had to be checked by using our fingers. The hens that did not have an orifice of sufficient size were removed, placed in chicken crates, and sold.

The degree of accuracy involved in this procedure depended on the skill and experience of the individual doing the checking. The only real check was by comparing egg production before and after culling. Dad did most of our culling, but some was done by a friend of the family who claimed some ability along this line. Although I assisted in this operation on a number of occasions, I did not seek expertise in this field; I found it about as unpleasant as the hens.

Keeping the Farm Running

Life on the farm involved numerous tasks in addition to daily chores and fieldwork. Some, such as hauling manure, extended periodically throughout most of the year, while others, such as gardening and butchering, were seasonal. All were necessary. A few are briefly discussed below.

HAULING MANURE

For obvious reasons, one of the least liked tasks was hauling manure. Since all animals had to be confined in shelters during the harsh winters, manure accumulated in large quantities and every attempt was made to remove it to the fields as soon as possible. Although the spreader could occasionally be used in the winter if the snow was not too deep, during this season most of the manure accumulated in the pens or on piles immediately outside the door of the shelter. It was removed in the spring when time and field conditions permitted. The machine used for this purpose was logically called a manure spreader.

Before the modern spreader was invented, farmers pitched their manure into single-box wagons and unloaded it in the field a forkful at a time, breaking up the larger lumps and spreading it about in the process. The spreader eliminated the work of unloading and performed the task in a more efficient manner by spreading the manure about evenly. Two horses were used to pull the machine and its mechanism was powered from the rear wheels. When activated, an apron in the bed of the vehicle moved the material slowly to the rear where beaters broke it into small pieces and cast it out into a swath behind the machine.

When nearly empty, our machine had a tendency to spread the material to the front as well as the back, which meant the operator also became a target. Attempting to reduce the target size, we would hunch over and cautiously peer around to see how much manure remained. Invariably, a juicy morsel would come flying our way and strike us directly in the face. The smell, and even the occasional taste, of wet manure smeared on a face is something best forgotten.

Unfortunately, the use of a spreader did not eliminate the physical task of loading; this remained a hand operation, using a tined manure scoop or a five-tined fork, depending upon the tensile strength of the manure. Straw, used as bedding, increased the fiber in the mix adding to its tensile strength. Every animal species made its own unique contribution to the cause, and we soon developed an expertise in identifying the unpleasant aspects of each.

Removal of the many small distinctively shaped droppings in the horse stalls was done with the use of the tined scoop. Whether due to an unusual digestive system or the enormous quantities of urine, a tremendous amount of ammonia gas was always present. Gnats and flies must have found the environment appealing because they lived there in countless numbers. They were not blood suckers; they preferred the tasty, moist morsels being exposed by our scoop, and during hot summer weather, a dense swarm of insects was always swirling about our heads. This ensured a closed mouth, squinting eyes, and very slow breathing through the nose.

The removal of cow manure from the barn was a daily task noted on page 69. The removal of the large pile outside the door was done in the spring as soon as the spreader could be operated in the field. As additional layers were added to this pile throughout the winter, they would freeze, and the pile would end up being a solid mass. During the removal, layers were peeled from the pile daily as they thawed out. This was done while standing knee-deep in mud that was adequately saturated with liquid manure. Although horse manure was also piled outside in winter, it never seemed to freeze into an impenetrable solid mass.

Removal of manure from the calf pens was difficult, but the

pig pens were the real hernia makers. As previously noted, hogs deposited their manure in one corner of their pen, invariably the one farthest from the door. It was thoroughly packed by their feet in a manner similar to sheep's foot compactors on soil embankments. Hog manure is naturally dense, but after daily compaction over a substantial period of time, it would have made a good foundation for a skyscraper. Every forkful had to be removed by straining the embedded fibers to the breaking point, and the heavy load had to be carried to the door and given a hefty heave into the spreader. The work always proceeded slowly, and in an environment of the most vile smelling animal waste known to man. Many references are made to horse, bull, and chicken manure in the cruder forms of our vernacular, but never to hogs. Since these references are meant to be derogatory in nature, it is difficult to understand why hogs aren't included.

Chickens are small, but the amount of manure they produced during the night, while sitting on their roosts, was not insignificant. Their droppings formed a ridge directly under each roost, with the height being directly proportional to the amount of time that had passed since the chicken house was last cleaned. When the elevation of this ridge reached a point where the chickens had difficulty getting to the roosts without wallowing in the deposits, it was time for another cleaning. The spreader was brought to the door, the 2″ × 2″ wood roosts were removed from their vertical supports, and the tined scoop put into action.

Because liquids and solids tend to be expelled together from the same orifice, chicken droppings are moist when they enter this world. However, they soon dry out and produce dust when disturbed, and this dust formed a dense, odoriferous cloud in the chicken house. The inhalation of this material was not pleasant, and when the weather was hot, it mixed with the sweat on our brows to form a most potent facial mud pack. Its high nitrogen content was good for plants in the field, but did little for the appearance of our face or our mental attitude. The task was best performed by holding our breath while dashing into the chicken house for a scoopful, and standing back to breathe again after pitching it into the spreader.

BUTCHERING

In the early 1900s many rural towns had their own small slaughter houses, but by the 1930s this was no longer the case. There were individuals who would butcher animals for local residents but most farmers did their own. Raising animals for market was a business, and knowing the fate awaiting them, we made no attempt to develop pets. However, after taking care of a group of animals from birth to maturity we developed a closeness and the butchering of these animals was approached with some degree of forced detachment. Necessity and the unsurpassed taste of fresh beef or pork gave us an incentive to proceed.

Since we had no refrigeration, our large animals, the cattle and hogs, were butchered during cold weather when the meat could be kept for a sufficient length of time to be consumed or prepared for preservation. Dad preferred beef, but lard was needed for shortening and at least one hog was butchered every year. Before economic conditions interfered, we butchered one steer and two hogs a year. There were some differences in the procedures involved with each.

The butchering of a steer began by choosing a medium-sized animal from those we were finishing for market, and leading it to the butchering site, where a .22 rifle bullet well-placed in the center of the forehead dropped the animal. Dad then stuck it by cutting the jugular vein to permit bleeding. When bleeding ceased, the steer was skinned and the carcass gutted by cutting open the intestinal cavity, reaching into the rib cage to cut the attachments, and pulling the entrails down and out. The liver and heart were removed and the rest given to the hogs.

The carcass was hoisted by using a block and tackle attached to a single tree and fastened to the tendons of the rear legs. The tongue was removed before the head was cut off and discarded with the entrails. After the front legs were cut off at the knees, the carcass was cut in half by splitting it down the back, using a knife, saw, and hatchet. The front quarters were detached from the rear quarters and taken to the north bedroom upstairs, where they were placed on sheets on the floor to cool. The rear legs were cut off at the knee and the rear quarters taken to join the front quarters. The hide was sprinkled with salt and tied into a neat packet to be sold.

Butchering continued after the body heat had dissipated. This would take a day or two, depending on the temperature in the bedroom. The quarters were then placed on the kitchen table (one at a time) and cut up into the desired sized pieces, using knives and a meat saw. Beef steak was, of course, the preferred cut, but all were packaged for early consumption or cooked and canned for later use. The heart, tongue, and other miscellaneous items were ground with a hand-operated meat grinder that was temporarily mounted on the kitchen table. This meat was used as hamburger or seasoned and used as baloney. We did not put our baloney into casements, although they could be purchased and a hand-operated tool used to fill them. The use of intestines for casements was diminishing, but I know of at least one relative who was still using them.

The butchering of a hog began by tying a rope around a rear leg of the chosen animal and herding it to the slaughtering site, where a hoist and a barrel full of hot water was waiting. The animal was wrestled to the ground where Dad stuck it while I held it. It was released with blood gushing from the open jugular. It would rise to its feet and take a few steps, but soon sank to its knees, and before long it was too weak to raise its head.

After bleeding, the carcass was hoisted and lowered into the scalding hot water in the barrel because this process facilitated the removal of hair from its body. This was done by hand, dipping each end of the hog into the barrel for a few minutes. After the dipping, hand scrapers were used to scrape the hair from its body. Next, the hog was carefully gutted and hoisted into the air by its back feet. The head was cut off, the front legs removed at the knees, and the resulting carcass cut in half. The rear legs were cut off at the knees and the halves taken to the house for cooling.

The cutting up and processing of a hog carcass differed somewhat from that of the steer. The hide was left on some parts for rind and the fat was cut into strips and put through the hand grinder to be rendered into lard. Rendering took place by boiling the fatty particles in a large container on the stove, and the hot grease was strained and poured into large crocks containing meat that had been previously cooked. The grease covered the meat and solidified into lard, preserving the meat. As the meat was later removed for eating, the lard was used for shortening. The solid pieces, remaining on the strainer and sometimes referred to as crackling, were fed to chickens or hogs.

Miscellaneous items were ground, seasoned, and made into uncased sausage. Mother was rather finicky and brains, lips, pigs feet, and such were not kept for human consumption. The women's role in butchering was not a minor one; their task, which included preservation of most of the meat for future consumption, continued long after the men's role was complete.

Later, at Manly, my parents had their butchering done for them. The meat was cut up and packaged to their specifications and put directly into a locker in town. (Lockers were walk-in freezers where farmers rented storage space. Vegetables and other items, such as strawberries, were also frozen and stored in them.)

BEES

We had honey bees when we lived at Lakota and they were moved to Ledyard and placed south of the house in the old orchard near the pasture. The number of active hives would change from year to year, but we usually averaged about six. Although the bees seemed to survive the severe winters quite well, occasionally a hive had to be replaced. I do not recall bees being purchased, but when a wild swarm was seen flying about in our vicinity, we got a large pan and beat on it like a drum. This seemed to encourage the queen bee to light on a tree limb or other convenient place where the workers could bunch themselves around her. (Perhaps the queen bee thought the drum sound was thunder and a storm was approaching.) A spare hive with the lid off was placed directly below and the swarm was shaken or prodded loose so it would drop into the hive. The hive was taken and placed near the other bees.

In the spring, the honey-retaining frames and dead bees were removed. The inside of the hives were briefly cleaned and newly prepared frames were placed into the hives. In the fall, some of the honey-filled frames were removed, leaving enough for the bees to survive on during the winter.

Preparation of the replacement frames to be inserted into the hives in the spring was a wintertime job. After frames were thoroughly cleaned, the edges of wax starter strips were melted and attached to the inside of the square openings where the honeycombs would be formed. Bees used these strips to start their combs.

Although there were a few occasions when Wilbur went door-to-door to adjacent farmers, selling combed honey, two pounds for twenty-five cents, we consumed most of our production. Combed honey was served at the table, but the liquid form with wax removed was preferred.

Honeybees were present in large numbers around blooming plants and sources of water, but they were not aggressive. They would freely walk over our fingers and would not sting unless squeezed or threatened. Occasionally, I would very carefully pick one up by pressing its wings together over its back; at such times, it would sting anything placed against its abdomen. They have a barbed stinger that cannot be removed easily from flesh or any other substances. After penetration, the bee remains permanently attached or has its stinger and entrails torn from its body, killing it. In this respect, they differ from other stinging insects that can sting repeatedly and not die in the process.

Their lack of aggressiveness did not extend to their homes. We could approach their hives without difficulty, but when the lids were removed and their interiors disturbed, the bees became literally mad. Because it was necessary to get into the hives twice a year, a screened, protective headpiece, long gloves, and a smoker were used when doing so. The smoker consisted of a metal chamber (in which a burning rag was placed), attached to an accordion-type base, which was "pumped" to blow air through the chamber, producing puffs of smoke. This smoke, blown into and around the hives, had a tranquilizing effect on the bees, so Dad or Wilbur could proceed with the work.

It should be noted that when someone was working around the hives, it was best for the rest of us to stay far away. Invariably, some bees were not tranquilized and these mad bees would attack us on sight. On one occasion, I was at the house, approximately one hundred yards away, when one struck my overall bib like a bullet and another struck a glancing blow on my arm. The stinger in the overall had penetrated through the denim and my shirt, puncturing my skin underneath. The one that struck my arm left a small, painful gash but no stinger. The glancing blow did not permit stinger penetration but it did leave its acidic deposit in the gash.

Dad's expertise with bees was not unknown. When a swarm of bees made its home in the attic of the manse at Lakota, Rev. Frerking asked him if he would remove them. Dad seldom got stung, but on this occasion two bees found their way around the protective head screen and stung him on the face. What made this particularly unpleasant was the fact that he could not remove the head screen to wipe the bees away because this would have permitted the entry of countless more. It must have been somewhat difficult to continue to work with two bees attached to his face by their stingers.

SAWING AND CHOPPING WOOD

The primary purpose for having a grove of trees around a farmyard was to provide a windbreak in the winter from the north and west, but the trees were also used to provide wood for heating and, in some cases, shade for man and beast. Our grove did not contain evergreens and was too thin to provide an effective windbreak, but it was a real lifesaver for the firewood and fence posts it provided. We had several different kinds of trees; maple, elm, and cottonwood were the most prevalent. Unfortunately, none of them provided the amount of heat good firewood like oak would have provided or had the rot-resisting quality of cedar.

Medium-size trees were chopped down with an axe and the larger ones were dropped by using a two-man saw. Those destined to become fence posts were cut into the proper lengths and hauled in a wagon to a pile where they were split into a size that would go into our post auger–size hole, which was done by using a thirteen-pound sledge and steel wedges. Those destined to become firewood were cut into lengths we could lift, hauled, and stacked near the buzz saw located north of the house. When firewood was needed, the tractor was used to power the saw to cut the logs into rounds that were approximately twelve inches in length. This had to be done with care; fingers were within inches of the large teeth on the rapidly rotating three-foot blade when holding the round as it was being cut off. This task was even more difficult and dangerous when the diameter of the log was larger than the radius of the saw blade and several cuts had to be made to get through the log.

MAKING FENCE

Northern Iowa was not open range country and every farmer was expected to fence his property to keep his animals confined. Each farmer was responsible for the right half of the property line fence as he faced his neighbor.

Aside from the specialty fences used for chickens, rabbits, and others, there were two kinds of fences in general use: barbed wire for cattle and horses, and woven wire for hogs. A good permanent barbed wire fence consisted of five tightly stretched strands stapled to cedar posts. A proper woven wire fence consisted of tightly stretched woven wire below and three barbed strands above, all attached to cedar posts. Cedar posts were used because they were more rot resistant and therefore more permanent. Steel posts were also in use, but they offered less lateral resistance than the wood and were generally used only for temporary fence or intermittently between wood posts in a permanent fence. We had a few steel posts, but no cedar, and we could not afford to buy new posts of any kind, so our grove became our source for fence posts.

The construction of a new fence began by placing the end posts first and the other posts were located in line by sighting along the posts. The distance between posts was paced off and the holes dug, using a post auger. This auger worked well in soil, but occasionally modest-size rocks prevented its progress.

To place the difficult-to-handle barbed wire along the fence line, one end of the wire from a spool was attached to an end post, a round steel bar was placed through the spool, and with a man at each end of the bar, we walked along the posts as the barbed wire unrolled from the spool. It was tensioned by using a block and tackle. When tightly stretched, it exerted a strong horizontal pull on the end posts, so they had to be adequately braced by struts and wires.

After making sure that the barbed strand was tensioned throughout its length and not hung up on the ground, it was attached to the posts at the proper height with staples for wooden posts and special wire ties for steel posts. Great care was necessary in nailing the first few staples. A sudden release of the wire by the stretcher was not unknown, and if anyone was holding the wire at the time, the barbs would race through hands like the teeth of a saw. To prevent injury, the barbed wire was always picked up by the claws of a hammer, or a staple puller, and held against the post while another hammer was used to drive home the staple. Once both ends of the wire had been securely attached, less care was necessary, but tightly stretched barbed wire was always treated with respect.

Woven wire was stretched by bolting two 2″ × 6″ wood pieces to the fencing and attaching them to the wire stretcher. Because it did not contain barbs, woven wire was not as dangerous, but it was also handled with care until securely fastened at both ends.

Posts consisting of soft wood rotted out at the ground line in a few years and replacing them was a never-ending task. When removing a fence, woven wire was easy to roll up, but barbed wire was difficult to handle. It was carefully rolled into large diameter hoops, and when reused, the same care was necessary. Much of our barbed wire was rusty and it would occasionally break, making the job difficult.

GARDENING

Farmers had always grown most of their own food and the depression intensified this practice. Gardens were large and the amount of necessary work was not insignificant. We had two gardens—one south of our garage in the new orchard area, the early garden, and one west of our grove. In addition to these gardens, we planted potato patches in our fields.

The women daily gathered fresh vegetables when in season, and since storage in our cellar did not prove feasible, those not immediately consumed were canned in fruit jars. Some of the early potatoes were dug up by hand, using a soil fork, but the main crop was harvested with a potato digger. This machine looked much like a walking plow. Its large shovel-shaped blade dug up the soil and placed it on a grate immediately behind, where a sprocket-spoked wheel vigorously shook the grate up and down as the team moved forward. The shaking forced the loose soil through and kept the potatoes on top, where they rolled off onto the ground. We picked them up, put them in buckets, and carried the full buckets to be emptied into a wagon.

We consumed large amounts of popcorn during the long winter evenings and its small ears had to be picked and shelled by hand. The time consumed in this pursuit was not insignificant.

WEED CONTROL

Plants that were out of place, more commonly referred to as weeds, were primarily controlled with use of our farm implements, including a single-row cultivator in our west garden, but some required the use of manual labor. Both gardens needed extensive hoeing and weeding, which meant plenty of work for all of us.

Our Ledyard farm had been blessed with a large number of cockleburs, a particularly obnoxious weed whose burrs became embedded in pant legs, shirt sleeves, and the tails and hair of horses and cattle. These burrs were not only inconvenient, they were painful and difficult to dislodge. Unfortunately, cultivation did not keep them in check and the only feasible solution was to pull the small plants out by hand as they appeared. Dolores joined the males in this unpleasant task, each of us taking two rows as we walked through the corn fields, stooping down for each cocklebur plant found. This procedure had to be followed in each field for two consecutive years before the number of plants diminished to insignificance.

The mower was used to cut weeds and grass along road ditches, but it could not be used immediately next to fence rows or in confined areas such as the grove. A scythe had to be used in these places. It had a bowed handle with two attached hand grips and a blade about twenty-eight inches long. Although Wilbur and I spent many hours using this tool, my clearest recollections are of Dad using it most every evening after supper as the sun sank slowly in the west.

SHELLING CORN

Ear corn was stored in cribs, but when sold to buyers in the elevators, it had to be shelled. This required the use of a sheller and we had to hire the services of an individual who had one. Later, shellers were mounted on trucks, but the first ones were small thresherlike machines that were towed. They were powered by belt and had a flexible-length dragline, cob unloading elevator, and a chute for discharging the shelled corn. Permanent corncribs were constructed with covered trenches in the floor where the dragline could be placed. The covers of these trenches were removed as required during shelling to permit the ear corn to enter. With temporary cribs, the dragline was placed adjacent to the crib and the corn pushed or shoveled into it.

The machine stacked the cobs in a pile nearby, and the shelled corn went into wagons or trucks to be taken to the elevators in town. Cobs were used for kindling, and frequently those who assisted in shelling took a wagonload home with them.

GRINDING OATS AND CORN

Oats were ground when fed to milk cows, small chickens, and piglets, and small amounts of corn were shelled by the hand sheller and ground for chicken feed. Ear corn was ground for milk cows and calves. The grinder, powered by our tractor, used eight-inch diameter steel plates to grind the various grains. These plates contained protrusions and indentations designed to grind the grain by rotating one plate against the other as grain was fed between them. The fineness of the grind depended on the force used to keep the plates together, which was adjustable. Grain was immediately fed to the plates after the grinder was activated since they would become red hot from friction if this was not quickly done.

PAINTING

To keep a large number of farm buildings attractively painted is not an insignificant task and is one that is now frequently contracted out. Renters seldom painted and landlords did not want to spend money on painting, so rented farms, such as ours before purchase, deteriorated rapidly. We painted our house and kept it in reasonably good condition even after we lost the farm, but the other buildings were not so honored. Painting was not to occupy much of our time until we lived at Manly later.

SHOVELING SNOW

The county eventually cleared our roads of snow, using snowplows, but making passageways through the snow on our yard was done by hand with a large grain scoop. In addition to footpaths for us, the cattle and horses needed access to the tank, and the driveway had to be cleared for the car. All males participated in this activity and the severe winter of 1935–1936 was one not soon forgotten. That year, keeping a lane open to the road for the car was especially trying.

MACHINE OPERATION AND REPAIR

After our move to Ledyard, no new equipment, cars, or machines were purchased, except for Mother's Dexter washer. In fact, the Whippet car and the corn picker, purchased around 1927, were the only machines purchased new while I lived at home, and the Whippet proved to be the last new car; they never purchased a new tractor. Consequently, I never experienced the use of new machinery and our old equipment had to be operated with care. Maintenance began taking more and more of our time, and except for occasional blacksmith work and two occasions when the Whippet was worked on briefly by a mechanic in Ledyard, all machine repair was performed by us at home. A brief description of a few of our machines and some of our experiences is worth mentioning.

Our Hart Parr had an engine that was lubricated with a dripper system consisting of six individual drippers in one box, each dripper dropping oil into tubes that led to various engine parts such as cylinders, crankshaft bearings, and connecting rod bearings. The oil was used but could not be recovered. The transmission was enclosed and had its own lubricant, but there were no grease fittings on the machine. The clutch was a brake band-appearing device that clamped over a drum surface on the exposed flywheel, and the fan was activated by a cone-shaped rubber wheel that was held against the side of the flywheel rim. The overhead valves had no valve cover, and the gears that turned the rear wheels were not enclosed and could not be lubricated because they were exposed to dirt. Our regular fuel was called distillate, although kerosene was also used when the price was right, and a small tank containing gasoline was used for starting.

To start the engine, the float bowl in the carburetor was drained, and the fuel valve turned to the starting tank (gasoline). The small cups in the cocks on top of the cylinders were filled with gasoline and opened. The ignition was retarded at the magneto. A large crank was inserted into the end of the crankshaft and the engine slowly turned over to draw in the gasoline from the cock cups. Eventually, the engine was rapidly turned over one compress stroke at a time by throwing body weight against the handle of the crank. When it started, the cocks were closed and the ignition was automatically advanced. If it started briefly and then stopped, the spark had to be retarded again before cranking or it would kick, which was a dangerous reaction under the circumstances. This happened once when Dad was cranking and the crank flew from his hands and struck the rear wheel, breaking a notch out of the cranking mechanism. When the engine had warmed up sufficiently, the fuel valve was turned to the regular tank (distillate).

If not completely warmed up when the fuel was switched to distillate, it was not unusual for the engine to stall, and the starting procedure had to be repeated. This was time-consuming, so the air cleaner pipe was detached from the carburetor and a large oil can containing gasoline was used to squirt small amounts of fuel directly into the carburetor intake whenever signs of stalling appeared.

Operation of this machine was not without its problems. When heavy pulling was involved, the front end of the tractor would rise slightly, making it difficult for the front wheels to grip the soil for turning. An angle, forming a sharp edge rim, was attached to the circumference of these wheels to assist them, but occasionally a turn at the end of the field was not started soon enough, and the fence would find itself resisting the advances of this iron monster.

Elements of danger were not lacking. The clutch was engaged by pulling vigorously backward on a large lever and on one occasion when Dad was plowing, this lever broke. Although he fell backwards onto the plow, he was able to extract himself and get back onto the moving tractor.

In addition to the usual minor repairs, there was one occasion when a broken piston needed replacing. Later, when no longer used for field work, the radiator failed and a steel barrel was mounted on the front in its place. By this time, the machine was fading fast and was about to join a pile of scrap steel at the local junk yard, a station stop on its way to reincarnation.

After the spring of 1929 our Model T Ford was no longer required for transportation to school, but we kept it as a second car until the motor was removed and put on the corn picker. This car was simplicity itself.

It had no water pump; the head of the engine was shaped to assist the less dense hot water to rise and enter the radiator at the top, and as the radiator cooled the water, gravity pulled it down (thermo siphon) and it reentered the engine block at the bottom.

It had no fuel pump; the gas tank was underneath the seat and gas flowed to the updraft carburetor by gravity. The lower part of the gas tank was little, if any, higher than the carburetor, and when gas in the tank was low, the engine stalled when climbing a steep hill. It was then necessary to turn the car around and back up the hill. The Model A, which followed this model, solved this problem by placing the gas tank at a higher elevation in front of the dash board. There was no gas gauge; the front seat had to be removed to get to the gas cap to put in gas, and a stick, provided for that purpose, was put in the tank to check the depth of gas.

There was no starter, generator (alternator), or battery; starting torque was manually applied by crank and a magneto provided the current for the ignition and lights. (The V-shaped magnets were incorporated into the flywheel as part of the magneto.) The ignition coils, one for each cylinder, were encased in wood and located beneath the dash. When the low voltage current from the magneto was applied to the primary of a coil, it activated an electromagnet that pulled the breaker points apart, which broke the circuit to the primary coil and induced a high voltage current in the secondary. This making and breaking created a buzzing sound and when generators and batteries were used in later models, this buzzing continued whenever the ignition switch was on and the engine was stalled at a point where a cylinder was to fire. The tone of the buzzing sound increased or decreased in frequency, depending on the setting of the points. This was the same system used on the Fordson tractor we had later. The magneto also provided the current for the lights, which meant that when the engine slowed down, the lights dimmed, and of course there were no lights when the engine wasn't running.

We had no side curtains for our car and the windshield wiper, which was only on the driver's side, had to be manually operated. There were two small levers under the steering wheel: one controlled ignition timing and the other was a gas feed. Although there was no gas pedal, the car had three pedals on the floor for controlling the "automatic transmission" and braking. When the left pedal was completely depressed, the transmission was in low or first gear. When it was partially depressed, the transmission was in neutral, and when fully back, it was in high or second gear. The center pedal was positioned slightly closer to the driver; when it was depressed the transmission was in reverse. The right pedal was the foot brake, which activated a brake band in the transmission.

To start the car, the two levers under the steering wheel were adjusted to retard the spark and open the gas feed, the hand brake was pulled back, which activated brake bands on the rear wheels and partially depressed the left pedal putting the transmission in neutral, and the operator then went to the front of the car to crank.

The crank was permanently fixed in a bracket immediately under the radiator; it was engaged by depressing it against a spring and turning it clockwise. A choke wire, projecting through the left side of the radiator, was used as required. Because current for the ignition had to be generated by the magneto, the faster the motor was turned over the easier it started, so most operators would spin the crank rapidly. If choking was required, the choke wire had to be pulled at the same time. Fortunately, the compression of the engine was such that starting the car was not difficult for a man to do. However, it was very important that the ignition be retarded because if it wasn't, the engine would kick and doctors would be kept busy, repairing broken arms. (This may be a reason so few women drove.)

When the motor coughed into life, black smoke poured from the mufflerless exhaust pipe with a roar that made hand signals a requirement for communication. The operator would dash from the front of the car and reach in to advance the timing and to adjust the gas feed to the desired speed. The entire vehicle shook vigorously, causing the many sheet metal parts to produce an unpleasant, loud rattling noise. The tin Lizzie was ready for action.

Because there was no door on the driver's side, the operator would climb over the left side or enter the vehicle on the right, place his left foot on the left pedal to keep it partially depressed to keep the car in neutral, and release the hand brake. While giving the car gas, the driver would push the left pedal to the floor, putting the car in first gear. After reaching a speed of approximately five miles per hour, he let the left pedal quickly back and the vehicle jerked into high gear. Acceleration was slow and the maximum speed was about thirty-five miles per hour.

The foot brake was adequate for the vehicle, but when a heavily loaded four-wheel trailer was being pulled, ample distance had to be provided for stopping. The reverse pedal could be depressed to assist in making an emergency stop, but this was a good way to assure the need for a major repair.

Our Model T did not give us serious trouble; I do not recall any need for major repairs. Even when the motor was later used on the picker, it performed without difficulty.

The evolutionary development of cars is evident when comparing the Model T with the Whippet, and the Whippet with later cars. The modern features possessed by the Whippet, such as four-wheel brakes, balloon tires, and glass windows, were pleasant to have, but there were deficiencies. Although it had a muffler, the motor was still quite noisy and became more so as it got older, which meant that conversation could only be carried out by shouting. (Even so, some young men used "cutouts" to increase noise—a valve installed in front of the muffler to bypass it.) Some of the Whippet's components left much to be desired as far as durability was concerned. It performed well the first few years, but soon after moving to Ledyard, the conditions of operation ensured the need for extensive maintenance and repair. A look at some of the more adverse operating conditions is in order.

The Whippet was our main form of transportation and it was used throughout the year. Getting stuck in the mud was not an unusual occurrence, and dirt roads did much to shorten the life of such vehicles, but operating them in cold weather proved to be most detrimental. Then the procedure was time-consuming and unpleasant.

There were no multiviscosity oils, so we used ten weight in the winter even though oil consumption went up with its use. Even so, when the temperature reached twenty degrees below zero, the viscosity of this oil was such that the starter could not turn the motor over. Even when temperatures were slightly higher, the six-volt system had such a voltage drop when the starter was engaged that the ignition was too weak to start the car. When this happened, a crank or a horse had to be used. Some people used kerosene to thin their oil, which was not a good practice. In the summer, heavier weights were used.

When cranking, the compression and stiffness of the engine made spinning impossible so the motor was turned over one compression stroke at a time by pulling up on the crank. It was easier to pull then to push, and if the motor should kick, there was less likelihood of breaking an arm. If the car refused to start when cranked, a horse was harnessed and used to pull it. The car was put in high gear (third), and the clutch depressed until it was moving. Because of the difficulty in turning the motor over, there were occasions when the rear wheels slid on the ground when the clutch was released.

After the motor started, the oil gauge was closely watched. Invariably, the oil was so thick that the pump could not circulate it. If so, the motor had to be stopped. A cob was soaked in kerosene, lit, and held under the oil pan, a task that could only be accomplished by lying on the ground and a most unpleasant task when in dress clothes. The motor was started again and the procedure repeated if necessary.

When oil pressure had been obtained, the temperature gauge had to be watched. We could not afford permanent antifreeze such as Prestone so methanol was used and this had a tendency to evaporate and raise the freezing point. When the mixture in the radiator froze, it couldn't circulate and the temperature of the motor would soon reach the boiling point. The motor had to be stopped, hot water from the tea kettle poured over the radiator, and the buffalo robe placed over the front of the car so the motor heat would assist in thawing out the radiator. When all conditions appeared ready, we proceeded down the road in low gear for half a mile or so until the viscosity of the grease in the transmission reached a point where shifting could take place while in motion.

There was no defroster on the car. Several different methods of defrosting were in use, including (1) a defroster glass temporarily attached to the windshield immediately in front of the driver, which resulted in a double pane with an air space between that reduced the problem; (2) electrical heating elements temporarily attached to the windshield; (3) a small fan mounted on the dash that directed warm air on the windshield; and (4) leaving the windows of the car partially open so that frost or fog would not accumulate on the inside of the windshield. The last method was the one we employed.

Glass-enclosed cars were so much warmer than the old isinglass curtains that heaters were not initially given much thought. Robes were still in common use. Later, a heater, purchased from the catalog for $3.75, was installed. It was a simple sheet metal device that enclosed the exhaust manifold and permitted the air from the fan to blow through it into the car. The device protruded through a hole in the dashboard and a simple gate valve controlled the amount of air entering the car. The amount of heat obtained by this device was limited, and fortunately, there were no leaks in the exhaust manifold or its gasket, which would have permitted carbon monoxide to enter the car.

Like most cars in operation, it had a vacuum-operated windshield wiper. The speed of these wipers was directly proportional to the vacuum in the intake manifold and since this vacuum decreased when the gas pedal was depressed, the speed of the wiper was inversely proportional to the amount of gas given to the car. When the gas pedal was pushed to the floor for passing, the wiper refused to work at all, resulting in the loss of wiper action when needed the most.

Tires and tubes were being improved, but flats were still quite common. Invariably, they occurred on a muddy dirt road. When a tire casing developed a hole or had been damaged in other ways, tire boots were often used to protect the tube so the tire could continue to be used. They consisted of cordlike tire material that was placed between the inside of the tire and the tube. They could be purchased in various lengths, some completely covering the inside of the tire, but most were smaller and used only at the damaged area. On at least one occasion, Dad made his own tire boots by cutting a piece out of an old tire and removing the tread. Wheel balancing was unknown and some front-end shaking was considered normal, but boots contributed more than their share to this undesirable reaction.

Wheel alignment was not considered critical. Toe-in was checked by using two yardsticks placed together to measure the distance between the inside of the tires of the front wheels. When the distance between the front of the tires was a fraction of an inch less than the rear, the wheels were aligned. Camber and caster were never checked.

The generator was driven by the timing chain and if not kept taut, the chain would slip a cog and throw the engine out of time. This was not an uncommon event and to prevent it, a wood block was shaped into a proper-sized wedge and placed between the generator and the motor block.

Gasoline was supplied to the carburetor by gravity from a small tank attached to the dash, and vacuum from the engine manifold was used to bring gas from the regular tank at the rear to this tank when the motor was running. When the car was not in use, the needle valve in the carburetor occasionally permitted the gas in the small tank to leak out and when gasoline in a small container was not available to put into this tank for starting, it was necessary for someone to go to the rear, remove the gas tank cap, and place his mouth over the opening and blow, maintaining a constant pressure in the tank while another person ran the starter. This procedure was not without interest when performed in public, and the party who did the blowing was instantly recognized by the dirt ring left as evidence around his mouth.

Either the cylinders in this engine were placed too close together or the head gaskets were inadequate because the gasket material between them frequently blew out. Whenever this happened, engine performance was not improved and head gasket replacement was necessary. On one occasion, a repair of the gasket was attempted by using solder but this did not prove feasible.

As use of the car continued, some teeth on the starter ring gear on the flywheel wore down so that the starter gear would slip when engaged at this point. It was necessary to turn the motor over slightly so there would be good teeth available to engage the starter gear. This could be done by using the crank or leaving the car in gear and pushing it slightly. When this procedure became so routine that people began to ask about our unique car, it was decided that the ring gear needed replacement.

A new one was ordered from the catalog. The transmission was removed, which was not an unusual procedure because it had to be done for clutch plate replacement, too, and the flywheel was removed from the motor. The flywheel and new ring gear were placed in a gunny sack and Dad carried them half a mile while walking with Wilbur toward Highway 9 at Gerled. From this point Wilbur carried them and proceeded alone. When he reached the highway, he hitchhiked the six miles to Swea City where he had a blacksmith grind off the old gear, heat up the new one, and place it over the flywheel to cool and shrink in place. He then hitchhiked back home and carried the flywheel the last mile. Finally, the car was reassembled with a renewed appreciation for good transportation.

As the car aged, the performance of the motor deteriorated, and it was finally decided that the pistons needed replacement. Oversized pistons and rings were ordered and taken with the car to a garage in Ledyard for installation. Piston removal was easily performed, but it was necessary to hone the cylinders to the precise diameter the new pistons required, and to do this, special tools were required—tools we did not possess. Apparently, the mechanic did not hone enough because we immediately had difficulty.

We assumed that we would have a powerful, smoothly running car after this overhaul and planned a pleasant, peaceful trip to Kamrar. This proved to be a mistake. The cylinders had been honed to a diameter where the pistons moved freely when cold, but not when hot. Driving a few miles to town did not create a problem, but after we had driven approximately twenty miles on our way to Kamrar, the pistons froze and we were stalled. We had to wait about forty-five minutes until the pistons cooled enough to permit us to turn the motor over with the crank. We proceeded another twenty miles and repeated the process.

As our trip continued, I recalled Mother telling me about a relative of ours who had made the trip from Kossuth County to Hamilton County by horse and buggy in three days. There was some doubt in my mind whether we would make any better time than they had. Fortunately, the time interval between stops soon increased as the pistons wore in, and we eventually arrived at our destination. It was not a trip we looked back on with fondness.

Not long before we were to part with this car, a fan blade broke off and penetrated the radiator. A new radiator was out of the question, so babbitt metal was melted and the hole in the radiator plugged with this molten metal. The performance of the heating system was not improved and greater care was necessary for operation of the engine.

In 1935 the Whippet was traded in on a used 1931, two-door Chevrolet that we purchased in Mason City, Iowa. I recall the total cost of the Chevrolet being $250, but how much they gave Dad for the Whippet is unknown. Whatever it was, it was too much because it had 45,000 miles on it at the time, and these were, indeed, hard miles.

As previously noted, our four-wheel trailer was homemade, constructed from the chassis of a junked car. Steering was accomplished by attaching the tie rods to its short tongue and a pin and clevis were used to attach the tongue to the towing vehicle. There were no lights or electrical connections and when used about the farm, no emergency chain attachment was used.

Caution was advised during towing. When traveling on a good road we would slowly accelerate up to thirty-five miles per hour. Invariably, whiplashing would occur and we would have to slow down to a crawl and start all over, slowly building our speed to something less than thirty-five miles per hour. At this reduced speed the vehicle was slightly more pacified and delayed its snake dance somewhat, but the pause was never permanent. When whiplashing returned, we repeated the process, always returning to a lower and lower speed. This continued until our maximum speed was perhaps ten miles per hour, and there was some doubt whether we were saving time by not using horses. Animals found riding in this vehicle most disturbing. When taken to the slaughter house, they left the wagon with pleasure, and there were occasions when we were tempted to join them.

The whiplash problem and the trouble in moving the box from wagon to trailer and back to the wagon led Dad to construct a two-wheel trailer out of the front axle of a car chassis. (The rear axle could also be used. When using the front axle, the tie rods had to be permanently attached in the correct position so the vehicle would trail properly. When the rear axle was used, there was more drag due to the differential.) Electrical connections were still not in evidence and a clevislike connection was used in lieu of a ball joint. An adequate emergency chain connection was now a permanent fixture. Although smaller than the four-wheeler, it was more convenient to use and could carry the same items; the additional trips required were not a problem. Consequently, the four-wheeler was seldom used again.

FUELS AND LUBRICANTS

Kerosene, occasionally referred to as coal oil, was in common use near the end of the 1800s, but cars and engines required gasoline and its use began slowly in the early 1900s. The public was aware of its highly volatile nature that resulted in violent flash ignition when starting fires, so storage and handling of this product was of some concern. In the beginning it was sold from barrels in bulk at hardware stores. I recall Dad telling me of one of his first experiences with it. A salesman explained that a container completely full of gasoline was not explosive, but became so as gasoline was removed. An empty, enclosed container that had previously contained gasoline was particularly explosive because the gasoline vapors that remained mixed with the air to form a dangerous and explosive mixture. The salesman demonstrated the less explosive nature of a full container by igniting one. After the initial flare up, the gasoline burned slowly and continued to do so until it was put out by removing its source of air. Storage outside was recommended and gasoline was *never* to be used to start fires.

Either a spout on the container or a funnel of sufficient size was required for putting gas in a car tank. Later, service stations appeared and the gas was dispensed directly into a car by use of a hose. Gasoline was pumped by hand from an underground storage tank into a calibrated glass container that was located on top of the pump, and the hose and a spout were used to let the gas flow by gravity into the car tank. No electricity was required for the pump's operation and the amount dispensed was shown by the calibrations on the glass. These pumps were in use through the 1920s and into the 1930s.

Farm tractors could not be fueled in town and the quantity of fuel used demanded a convenient means of delivery. Tank trucks soon made their appearance and came into general use. They delivered not only distillate for tractors, but also gasoline, kerosene, motor oil, and axle and cup grease. Fuels were dispensed into five-gallon containers at the rear of the truck by a series of valves, one for each type of fuel. The containers hung from the valves as they were being filled, and the quantity delivered was determined by the number of containers filled.

The explosive nature of gasoline dictated the use of an automatic grounding device to short out static electricity and a metal chain hanging from the rear of the truck served this purpose. The end of this chain bounced along the road surface when the truck was in motion, and when traveling on concrete or gravel, sparks were frequently emitted. The noise it made while bouncing along the road was generally louder than the truck and always alerted us of the approach of the tank truck. Although it no doubt served its purpose of preventing the buildup of static electricity, the sparks it made on the road surface made us wonder if there wasn't a better way.

Our gasoline was stored in a large steel barrel that sat on its end on top of a wood support in the garage. The spigot at the bottom was high enough to permit the filling of the five-gallon can that we used to put gasoline into the various machine tanks.

Distillate was stored outside in several steel barrels that sat on end on the ground where the tractor could approach them. A rotary hand pump was inserted in the barrels to pump their contents directly into the tank on the tractor. This rotary pump had a threaded tapered tap that fit the various sized holes in our steel barrels. Kerosene was also stored in a barrel located near the others and in an elevated position for ease in dispensing.

Bulk oil in barrels was dispensed in the same manner as that used in the oil stations. The crank handle of a hand-operated oil pump that had been inserted into the barrel was rotated in a counterclockwise direction until it stopped; then it was rotated in a clockwise direction, spurting oil until one pint had been dispensed, at which point the handle stopped. A one-quart, open oil can with an attached spout was generally used to put oil directly into the car or tractor. Numerous small oil cans were used to oil the other machinery; many machines carried their own oil cans. Grease gun fittings were coming into use and we had them on the Whippet, but it was the only machine on our farm so equipped. Its alemite system did not work as well as the zerk now in use.

Cup grease came in gallon-size buckets and was put into the cups by using a small wood paddle that came with the grease. When a grease cup was full of grease and screwed down onto the fitting, grease was forced into the bearing. As the machine was used, the cup was periodically given a few turns.

Axle grease came in larger buckets and a larger paddle was used for its application. Hub nuts on wagons were square, and a wrench to remove them was generally incorporated into the pin used to attach the eveners to the tongue. The nuts on the right side of the wagon tightened in a clockwise direction and those on the left counterclockwise, which was the direction of rotation of the wheels as the wagon moved forward and tended to keep the nuts from coming off. Wheels were greased by removing the nut, lifting the wheel, and pulling it off part way. The paddle was used to apply a liberal amount of grease to the large tapered axles.

Socializing and Health Care

GROOMING

The extensive physical labor we engaged in during the typical hot, humid Iowa summers generated a great deal of sweat, and after seven days the resulting residue contained countless bacteria, which generated sufficient odors of an undesirable nature to make a bath mandatory before contact with other humans. This Saturday night activity was a prerequisite necessary for our reentry into society. Cleaning up was not an involved activity but we were not entirely without vanity and grooming with our elementary facilities was sometimes challenging.

There were six of us and no bathroom, so a high degree of coordination and timing was required. Water was pumped and carried from the well to the house and heated in a boiler on our range, and the quantity required for six individuals was not insignificant. In the summer baths were taken in the shanty and were not unpleasant, although they were hastily performed because we wanted to get to town.

In the winter we bathed in the kitchen after supper. Because the temperature of this room quickly returned to that which existed outside, the procedure was performed with amazing speed. When my long underwear came off, an arctic blast struck my naked, shaking body with a vengeance, and since the warm water was not deep enough to submerge in, my bath, taken in a round, galvanized metal tub, frequently consisted of using a wet wash cloth to dab strategic spots. The towel was quickly employed and clean long underwear was soon in place. A rapid exit was made to the living room, where I stood shaking by the heating stove as I finished dressing.

The practice of men being shaved by barbers in town had not entirely disappeared and Saturday night saw men waiting at the barber shop for shaves and haircuts. However, I do not recall Dad joining this group; he had a straight edge and did his own, with Mother using the razor to trim the back of his neck. A leather sharpening strap was temporarily hung by the wash basin and boiling water was put into a shaving mug that contained a round bar of soap. A small round brush was used to lather the face and neck. Shaving was not an act regularly performed during the week, unless a special event presented itself.

We had a hand-operated hair clipper that Dad used to give us haircuts and Mother used on him. (I was not to experience the services of a barber until I left home.) The clipper was, no doubt, designed and constructed by a sadistic fiend who never intended to have it used on himself. Clipper action was provided by the hand as it was moved across the skull and if the forward action exceeded the clipping action, hairs were not sheared off, but were removed by pulling. The ratio of pulled to sheared hairs was directly proportional to how soon Dad wanted to finish the task, and he always seemed to be in a hurry. Although my ancestors have been accused of being responsible for the baldness some of us enjoy, I am convinced that our hair follicles just gave up trying to keep up with this instrument of torture. We soon developed a liking for long hair.

While lacking in style, the resulting coiffure was more than adequate for its time. I recall no adverse comments, which may well have been due to the unlimited range of unique haircuts on public display; the bowl-on-the-head approach was not unknown among those who cut their own.

It is an irrefutable law of nature that those who have straight hair prefer the curly or wavy variety, and those with curly hair prefer straight. Since no ancestor of mine back to antiquity was known to have a kink in his or her hair, I preferred the wavy kind. To acquire such a shape temporarily on my limited resources required extensive work and the liberal use of hair oil. This colorful product was purchased in bottles for ten cents, and a sufficient amount was put on to saturate the hair so it could be slicked down with a slight wave locked in place. This drowned rat appearance was supposed to convince those who casually glanced my way that I had naturally wavy hair. The oil was somewhat perfumed to make its presence more acceptable, but its lubricating qualities were not admired by Mother when it entered my starched shirt collar. I recall no instance where hair oil aided me in any relations with anyone but the hair oil salesman.

Dolores was now at an age where she considered the appearance of her hair extremely important and she periodically used a gooey, smelly substance made from flax to create some degree of waviness. This substance would dry in place and when finally removed, leave her hair in an exhausted and undulated shape. Unfortunately, the hair soon reverted to its original shape and the process had to be repeated.

One day she came home from school and told Mother that the girls in her class were getting permanents and she needed to have one, too. This is the first occasion I heard this expression used for a hair treatment and I had visions of one that would last forever. After a few weeks of persuasive arguments, Mother was convinced that this treatment was, indeed, a necessity for the maintenance of Dolores' social standing and she arranged to get a permanent for her on Saturday at Buffalo Center, the closest place where appropriate facilities were available. The permanent cost one dollar. The next Monday, Dolores proudly displayed her permanent to the other girls in her class, few of whom had ever had one.

Permanents did not prove to be as permanent as I had supposed. Dolores's hair gradually returned to a linear shape and she expressed her need for another one. Farmers were not known for their propensity to take their daughters to town for hair treatments, and Dad was in no mood to set such a precedent, so such trips did not become numerous. However, the seed had been sown and the inevitable could not be resisted forever; the need for women to go to the beauty parlor was soon to become an accepted part of feminine behavior.

We were not fashion conscious in the sense that the latest catalogs were eagerly snatched up for the purpose of observing the latest styles. We obtained new clothes when we outgrew or wore out our old ones, and a new look did not mean a change in style. Mother made some dresses and no doubt had a pattern in mind. Frills were obviously in short supply but I do not recall a sack look just because the cloth had previously contained feed.

I had two different kinds of clothes: overalls and a dress set for church activities. The dress set included a suit, white shirt, dress shoes, and overcoat when required. The newest overalls were for school and visiting, and the older ones for work. No doubt the expression "clothes make the man" is an exaggeration, but I found it difficult to strut around in overalls, pretending to be an important dude. My best opportunity to strut was with my dress clothes.

Mother liked knickers and I was doomed to wear these monstrosities until I was thirteen years old. When wearing these "bloomers," I felt extremely self-conscious and partially undressed, and the fact that another member of my Sunday school class had to wear them too did little to reduce my disdain for them. The appearance of the lower portion of my anatomy when wearing long underwear and knickers was, fortunately, never recorded on film.

My entry into the adult world of long trousers took place when I confirmed in the Presbyterian church. I soon became somewhat fashion conscious and joined others of my age in dressing up in a manner prescribed by my contemporaries. Having no other time to show off our finery, every Sunday became the occasion for an Easter parade. Polishing our Sunday shoes before going to church was a routine as natural as breathing, and in the summer when I wore white shoes, the scuffing they were subjected to dictated the use of large quantities of white polish. Spats were in vogue during this period and the buttons on these accessories were fastened with the use of a hook in a manner similar to women's high-button shoes.

Ties were mandatory, of course, and no man was dressed unless he had a collar clasp and tie pin. These silver- or gold-colored accessories were not the expensive kind; the quality was comparable to the gifts found in Crackerjacks, but diamonds could not have enhanced their value to us.

In the winter, survival dictated the use of overcoats and gloves, and a scarf was essential. The scarf could be composed of silk or wool, but it had to be used in the prescribed manner—wrapped around the neck and tied in such a way that it bulged out under the chin just the right amount. One then had the appearance of a diplomat on his way to a high-class social affair ready to dispense with a few frivolous comments.

Inclement weather did not make it easy for us to wade through mud or snow in a dignified manner. Overshoes and rubbers were used as required as large quantities of mud were never particularly welcome. We did not use umbrellas; I recall few of them in use.

Overalls and work shoes were not subjected to whims of fancy and did not change in appearance, but there was one occasion on which I talked the folks into getting me a pair of high-top boots. These boots were my pride and joy until they wore out, at which point I cut the tops off and used them as high-top spats. I do not recall establishing a fashion trend, however.

It should be noted that dressing up for Dad included wearing a suit, a white shirt with sleeve garters to keep his shirt sleeves from protruding beyond his coat sleeve, cuff pins, and garters for his socks.

SATURDAY NIGHT

On Saturday night during the summer, virtually all farmers went to town. This was the only get-together where everyone mixed, and the street was the place of meeting. It was not a fashion parade in the sense that everyone dressed up—most did not—but was more of a meet-the-neighbors gathering. Many women, including Mother, preferred to remain in the car and watch the people stroll by, but this required a parking spot on Main Street and to get one of those, we had to be early. The only way to be early meant stopping fieldwork and doing the chores sooner than usual, something we managed to do, unless we were at a critical point in harvesting.

Saturday night activities also included a band concert. Early in the evening, the bandstand was towed and parked at the main intersection of town so those who wished could stand on the street to listen. Because the main business district was only two blocks long, everyone within the area could hear the music. Conversations were not curtailed during these musical presentations and complaints about prices and damning the government were the usual means of maintaining verbal interaction with acquaintances.

After the band concert, the bandstand was towed back to an empty lot and the young men started driving up and down main street, exhibiting their driving finesse. Because the drive was only two blocks long, the time element involved was not great, so the process had to be repeated over and over. No one had a sports car or hot rod, but young dudes impressed local damsels by driving the family car at speeds that subjected it to stresses and strains for which it was not designed.

As a small child, I got five cents on Saturday night, which would get me an ice cream cone, candy bar, or popcorn. This was not an allowance, and I did not get it during the winter. Later, I received ten cents, which allowed me to see a movie at the theater. When I attended the movie, I could not enjoy a tasty treat, of course, but this was generally my choice. I attended my first movie—*The Bird of Paradise*—in April of 1933, when Dolores's confirmation class went to Algona to have its picture taken.

Law enforcement in town was not a problem. I do not recall any occasion where there were difficulties of sufficient intensity to require an individual's arrest. I was informed that a man in Lakota had been appointed to keep the peace on Saturday nights, but there was never a uniform in evidence. (I recall seeing a uniform for the first time on a Highway Patrol officer after they were established in the 1930s.) Because it was thirty miles away in Algona, the county jail was rather inaccessible, although the youths I associated with were of the opinion that there was a room in the small structure by the water tower where a person could be temporarily confined if the need arose. But I do not recall its ever being used.

RELIGIOUS ACTIVITIES

My parents were very religious and Sunday was God's day, a day of rest. No unnecessary work was performed and attendance at all church activities was mandatory. I know of no case where we did not attempt to go to church, even if a team was required to pull the car to the highway.

I faintly recall attending the Presbyterian church in the old wood building while the basement of the present church was being constructed, and later attending services in the basement of the new church while the superstructure was being built. Rev. O. H. Frerking came as pastor in 1928 and he remained in this position as long as we lived in Kossuth County. He and Dad had been at the seminary in Dubuque at the same time and were old acquaintances. Dad served the church as a trustee.

Each spring before Easter, the members of the new confirmation class became members of the church and in our family this introduction into full membership was taken for granted. Mine was to take place in 1935, with several months of religious instruction in catechism on Saturday afternoon preceding the event. Rev. Frerking was the catechism instructor and after the successful conclusion of each class, he would take members to some nearby city for an official photograph and to see a movie. Our class was taken to Mason City, and I recall our entrance to this metropolis over the cobblestones of North Federal. For me, this city was a very large one indeed.

HOLIDAYS

Birthdays were not a big affair in our family. My parents paid no attention to theirs and we were not to honor them on this day until we were older and had our own families. For the children, there might be a little fancier dinner, but gifts were restricted to necessary clothing. However, we did have two aunts, Gertie and Bertha, who sent us a small gift on this day, and we looked forward to this with great anticipation. I recall waiting patiently for the mail on the days immediately preceding my birthday until the toy arrived.

Although not national in scope, the annual Sunday school picnic was an event of equal importance to us. At first, it was held at a suitable site in the vicinity of Lakota, but later a more grandiose environment was required and an amusement park such as Arnolds Park at Lake Okoboji was the usual choice. A potluck lunch was served and some games were played, but most activities involved the amusement park.

Washington's birthday, Memorial Day, and Armistice Day (now Veteran's Day) were of little concern to us, but such was not the case with the Fourth of July. (We never referred to it as Independence Day.) This was, indeed, a special day. Fieldwork was suspended and a trip to Arnolds Park at Lake Okoboji was in order. Mother prepared a picnic lunch and at the park we were free to go roller skating, swim, or participate in whatever amusements we could afford.

Being at a lake, swimming was obviously one of the more popular activities, but I did not know how to swim, so wading and splashing water was my limit. I had no swimsuit, so I wore summer underwear with a strategically placed safety pin. It performed adequately except for one unexpected occasion when my safety pin came loose and exposed me to much humiliating laughter.

We never went out to eat in restaurants, so eating hamburgers or hot dogs and drinking pop was an activity we greatly enjoyed. The weather was always hot and a substantial part of my money always went for drinks. On one occasion, it appeared that I had found a solution to this problem—a soft drink stand that sold a twelve-ounce glass of orange drink for five cents or all you could drink for ten cents. I was thirsty and sure that I could drink two glasses, but if I delayed and let my thirst intensify, the all-you-can-drink option would prove to be a more profitable one. This was the option I chose.

Periodically, I strolled by the stand and calculated how many glasses I could drink. As the cotton in my mouth increased, the count kept rising, and after what seemed to be an eternity, the limits of my endurance were reached at the count of eight. I approached the stand, laid my dime on the counter, and said, "All I can drink."

I gulped the first glass down and was rather surprised how much it quenched my thirst; I reduced my estimate to seven. The next glass went down somewhat slower and when I finished it, I was no longer thirsty. However, I was not about to stop; my estimate was now six. The following glass was downed very slowly, the last portion being somewhat forced; my count was then five. When I placed the empty glass on the counter again, I must have appeared somewhat distressed because the attendant filled it half full and said, "Try this first." Every swallow of this glass was forced down like the handle of a tire pump, increasing the pressure in my stomach with each stroke. When the glass was empty, the count was over and I staggered away with a certain degree of discomfort, but with that warm feeling that follows a successful business transaction. I had proceeded about ten feet when my stomach exploded and orange drink shot from my mouth like a ball from a cannon, striking a bystander on his pant legs and shoes. That warm, pleasant feeling instantly departed and was replaced with panic. I made a hasty retreat, not looking back for the reaction of those left behind. This stand never saw my presence again.

The one aspect of the Fourth of July holiday that differed from all others was the use of fireworks. Funds for this activity were limited, but I always managed to get a number of firecrackers, mostly one-inchers and a few two-inchers. Consequently, for a few days my spare time was spent determining the destructive nature of these objects under different conditions. Various length fuses were experimented with and occasionally a two-incher went off in my hand. This trial and error approach sometimes resulted in injury to my fingers but not of a serious nature. The use of these objects to disturb others was not unknown, and on one occasion at a lake, I performed such a task above and beyond the call of duty.

I was strolling along the beach, looking for objects to blow up when I found a dead fish. It had obviously been dead for some time, but the distinctive odor of its ripeness was not apparent until approached closely; therefore, it did not disturb the rather large crowd enjoying a picnic lunch at a nearby table. This happy scene was about to change. I decided a two-incher was needed to thoroughly spread the fish's essence about and proceeded with the detonation. The results were well beyond my expectations and the stench was such that I made a hasty retreat, which proved to be a wise decision. The picnic crowd dispersed with great speed and the people were soon looking for someone who looked like me. I spent the rest of the day ensuring my good health by making sure they did not see me.

Thanksgiving was not an important day for us. I enjoyed two days off from school but frequently we were still picking corn, and this activity replaced the academic environment. The only festive aspect of the occasion was a more elaborate dinner. We never had turkey. Mother always fixed chicken, an extra side dish or two, and pumpkin pie—the only significant recognition of the holiday.

Christmas was the holiday of holidays. Various sequential events took place leading up to the big day.

In order to ensure the selection of the most preferred gift within the acceptable close-to-a-dollar price range, a thorough study of the Sears and Roebuck, Montgomery Ward, and Spiegel catalogs began weeks in advance. This price limitation reduced my search to restricted portions of the catalog, but planning and anticipation is supposed to provide 90 percent of the enjoyment associated with such occasions, and the small size of the gift did not materially dampen my enthusiasm. I would zero in on an appropriate gift in sufficient time to make its purchase, and it was the one I usually received.

At Ledyard, the first Christmas event outside of school took place on the last Saturday afternoon before Christmas. Town authorities held a drawing for a large prize and sacks of candy were distributed to the children. One year the prize was a small Ford auto, and naturally the most affluent man in town got it.

The next event was a Christmas Eve program at church. All the young children participated in this affair, most becoming quite angelic in the process. Except for Easter, this was the only event where the capacity of the church was insufficient; all parents wanted to see their darlings perform in public and there wasn't a Presbyterian within thirty miles not in attendance, as well as many others of dubious religious affiliations. The performances were somewhat less than professional, but out of the mouths of babes came a naturalness pleasant to the ear, even if not always according to the script. There was always a large Christmas tree in the sanctuary and at first candles were used to light it up, but a fire during one of these programs convinced those in charge to use electric bulbs in the future. At the conclusion of the program, sacks of candy and nuts were distributed to the children, and this generally included those who would never see twenty again. Afterwards, we headed for home and bed, emotionally charged for the next morning.

After we went to bed Christmas Eve, the folks placed our presents on the dining room table. The first child up the next morning made a sufficiently loud dash downstairs to awaken the others, and soon all were actively involved in manhandling presents, not only those from our parents, but also those from Ben and Gertie, and Bertha and Able. Nuts and candy were in abundance and the day was one of celebration and leisure.

For my parents and the small children, New Year's Eve was just another night, but the church had a program to assist young people in welcoming in the New Year. Dancing and the consumption of alcoholic beverages were not a part of these affairs and I recall no complaints about the evenings of games being too boisterous.

New Year's Day was uneventful because as the day neared an end, unpleasant thoughts of school returned.

CARNIVALS

Carnivals seldom made their appearance and amusement rides associated with them were generally restricted to county fairs and events such as Sauerkraut Day. Occasionally during the summer, adjacent small towns would have a temporary roller skating rink, dance hall, or tent show. When these activities could be observed without charge, we frequently went. Although there were a few occasions when I participated in the roller skating, the dance hall was forbidden territory. I do not recall seeing a tent show, but I do remember seeing the tent for such a show as it was erected at Lakota. The roustabouts made the driving of tent stakes a united affair—encircling the stake, they each took a turn in sequence swinging a mallet to drive in the stake.

SAUERKRAUT DAY

In the latter part of summer, county fairs were held after small grain had been harvested. Many small towns also held festive events during this time, featuring such activities as carnival rides and tent shows. Kamrar had its Harvest Home Festival, Buffalo Center its Buffalo Day, and Lakota its Sauerkraut Day. I did not have an opportunity to go to any of these events except for Sauerkraut Day, and to me this was an event of extreme importance. It was here, and only after I was ten, that I had a peek at an outside world I knew little about.

When the big day arrived, Dad took me to town in the forenoon, gave me twenty-five cents, and left me on my own. He then went home and returned in the evening with Mother after they had completed chores. I then received an additional small stipend. However, while on my own, I would look for some friend to associate with and we would proceed up and down Main Street, which was the midway, observing and participating in the concessions to the extent that our finances permitted.

During the earlier part of the day, many of the tent shows were still in the process of being erected and it was in this setting that I first saw a black person. He was such a novelty to me and my friend that we treated him as a spectacle, periodically walking by to observe him in action.

One occasion provided me with my first opportunity to work for pay. Billy Smith and I were strolling by a man who claimed to be some kind of mystic fortune teller. He was just beginning to set up his tent when he offered us twenty-five cents to assist him. We thought he meant twenty-five cents each. We agreed and proceeded to get his paraphernalia and erect his tent. When we were finished, he said he had no money to pay us and that we would have to come back later after he had made some. We had no choice so we left and returned about an hour later when he repeated the same sad tale.

Bill and I were to repeat this process until early in the evening when the man apparently got tired of our periodic appearance. He said he would give us all the money he had—twenty-one cents—just to get rid of us.

On another occasion, another friend and I became intrigued with a show called the "Wild Man from Borneo." (Apparently it was capitalizing on the publicity of the Johnson explorers and the beast they had captured in Borneo.) As we periodically walked by this stand, the barker would go into his loud spiel about the wild man who ate live chickens. Eventually, we were convinced that our future lives would be unfulfilled if we missed this rare opportunity to see a show of such worldwide significance, and we paid our money and went inside.

Within the small tent was a square, roped-off area with a man, dressed in dirty rags, lying on the floor. He had claws attached to his hands, a long-haired wig on his head, and he was painted to look like a beast. There were perhaps six of us in the tent when the barker came in, closed the tent flaps, and handed a live chicken to the wild man.

The beast on the floor literally tore the wings from the bird and pretended to eat them while actually stuffing the bloody parts under a loose shirt collar. He proceeded to tear off the chicken's legs and head, and rip open its body. After these parts had disappeared behind his shirt, he was a bloody mess and the show was over. We were immediately shown to the exit door.

Carnival rides were very much a part of these affairs; the merry-go-rounds and Ferris wheels were always a must. My first view of what was referred to as a loop-the-loop ride was on a Sauerkraut Day at the south intersection of the midway. This hammer-shaped machine was very similar to many now in use. The riders sat in the head of the hammer as it was rotated vertically about the end of its handle. A friend and I had been viewing this ride with interest and some apprehension. We finally decided that because there were no viewers about, we would make the plunge and give it a try.

The ride was pleasant as it began to swing back and forth, but as it got higher and higher, our laughter subsided and concern appeared. When we reached the point where we began to hang upside down on the upward swing, our hands were clutching the bar support with all our strength and my friend asked the operator to stop. He refused and we went higher and higher until we were hanging upside down on the top. At this point, my friend became extremely vocal and began to yell for help, continuing to yell until the operator stopped the machine.

This yelling was, no doubt, heard throughout the two-block midway and as we stepped out, we saw the Telkamp twins standing on the corner, doubled over with laughter. There was a quick silent communication between my friend and me and we turned and hurriedly left in the opposite direction. For the rest of the day, I kept my eye open for the twins. I had no desire to get into a long philosophical discussion concerning the relative merits of a ride on the loop-the-loop.

Some of the stands sold products not available in stores and I recall one that appeared to be highly successful in selling its unique product. It was at night and the crowd around the stand made getting close impossible, but the barker's spiel could be heard by everyone. He claimed his magic, bottled potion would cure every ailment known to man, including faulty regularity, a claim no medicine ignored. He also claimed his potion would make every consumer more attractive to the opposite sex. The regular price for this highly prized product was fifty cents a bottle, but he so admired the people of Lakota that he was offering it at a greatly reduced price, "fifty percent off or twenty-five cents a bottle, your choice." Sales were brisk and I recall one young man, impatient to improve his appearance, got his bottle and immediately took a good swig. Sure enough, his back straightened up and he was holding his head high as he disappeared into the crowd. There was some doubt in my mind whether my physical appearance had reached the highest degree of perfection obtainable and I was about to get in line and purchase a bottle when it occurred to me that I was out of money. My pursuit of snake oil had to await for more affluent times.

OTHER SOCIAL CONTACTS

Contacts with people outside of our family, other than those noted, were few and far between. Sunday afternoons were for visiting, and we continued this activity, but we did not have a phone so our visits were made unannounced. There were a few locals who met at stores during the winter and sat around a stove to talk, but Dad was seldom one of them. However, going to another farm and negotiating the services of a male pig was an event not soon forgotten, and attendance at nearby farm sales was a must. These were not auction sales of the farm itself but a sale of machinery and personal possessions by people who were leaving the farm. The purchase of a twenty-five cent hay fork or a box of tools for fifty cents was the limit of most of our transactions.

The only farm organization of importance in our community was the Farm Bureau, and my parents were members of this organization for a number of years. A metal sign attached to our gate post noted that we were members of this organization and indicated that the bureau would offer a reward for the conviction of anyone stealing from the premises. Although my parents were not active and seldom attended meetings, I do recall one held at our place.

Our house was too small for a gathering of this size, so Dad built a temporary platform on the east side of the house, where the speakers could talk while others sat in chairs on the lawn. Dolores provided the musical portion of the program by playing a selection or two on the piano, and a lunch followed the main program. The extent of the crowd convinced Mother and Dad that future meetings should be held elsewhere.

Door-to-door salesmen were not restricted to urban communities. Some, like the Watkins and Raleigh men, were welcome. Purchases of medicinal items such as salves and consumable items such as bottles of nectar concentrate were frequently made. These salesmen carried their supplies into the house for display and a leisurely visit usually followed. Other peddlers, traveling in various types of covered wagons, were not always welcome. On one occasion, one of them was seen picking up junk in our grove upon his departure, and he was told not to make another appearance on our farm.

HOME REMEDIES AND MEDICAL TREATMENTS

The term "preventive medicine" was not in use, but there were substances ingested for this purpose and they were not in short supply. A few involved the use of over-the-counter items, not the least of which was a small pill sold under the name of Carter's Little Liver Pills. The liver's importance in the scheme of things led to the consumption of an astronomical number of these pills and no home was without them. Of course they aided regularity, but their most beneficial use for me, may well have been as a placebo, inducing my mind to assist in the maintenance of good health.

Vitamins were unknown to us, but there was the wretched tasting cod liver oil that supposedly aided digestion, and I, being inclined to sickness, received regular doses. It was ordered from the catalog and given to me at the table in front of the rest of the family after supper. I can think of no greater appetite reducer than the thought of having to top off a meal with a large tablespoon of this viscous, extremely fishy, liver extract. It had a tendency to make me gag, but Mother had no desire to see me put my meal back on the table and another spoonful would soon follow if such were my reaction. Superhuman effort was used to keep it down until food diluted its gagging qualities. I always hoped Dad would forget to give it to me or forget to order more when the bottle was empty, but this was never to be the case. As the level of the fluid approached the bottom of the bottle, my spirits rose, but invariably, just before the last spoonful, another unwelcome package would arrive in the mail.

When taking these substances did not prevent ailments, stronger measures were required, the first was the purging of the lower digestive system. Although this was accomplished in children by the use of castor oil, adults never seemed to use it; they were more inclined to use Nature's Remedy. The taking of this frothy oil was as disagreeable to me as the taking of cod liver oil, but its effects later were substantially different. My bowels were supposed to move, and move they did, frantically trying to remove this bean extract. There were other, more pleasant-tasting laxatives, such as Ex-Lax, but medicine was supposed to taste bad, no doubt to prevent the appearance of pseudoillnesses that a patient might use to escape unpleasant tasks.

There were, of course, ailments and physical difficulties that did not lend themselves to the treatment noted above. Colds required only the use of Smith Brothers cough drops. These bearded brothers' product was preferred over the triangular-shaped mentholated Vicks because they tasted more like candy. Sore throats and chests were wrapped with a kerosene-soaked stocking, assisted with some mentholated salve. Earaches were treated with hot oil, generously poured into the ear in the hopes that something would break and permit the release of matter. Muscular soreness was treated with Sloans Liniment or Bay Rum; the burning sensations they produced soon made any user forget the soreness. Severe sunburn required an anointment of vinegar, and small wounds received an application of iodine; the stinging of the alcohol in this mixture on an open wound made it unpopular.

Slivers were common and were extracted with a minimum amount of surgery. If they resisted, we let them fester a few days until they were easy to pull. Stepping on rusty nails was a periodic occurrence when going barefoot in the summer, but no treatment was advised. Fortunately for us, these rusty objects did not contain the anaerobic organisms that have a reputation for locking jaws.

Athlete's foot was an occupational hazard when using the school gym and my feet proved to be a receptive haven for a particularly virile strain. Several treatments were tried, including boric acid powder, but to no avail. There were occasions when I took my shoes off when working in the field and on one occasion, I did so while hauling bundles during threshing.

Fortunately, no one in our family was ever seriously hurt, and with the possible exception of my left arm, no one ever broke a bone. At least I think I broke a bone because I have a two-inch bone spur on my upper left arm that army doctors later informed me appeared to be caused by a fracture. When I asked Mother about this she informed me that at a young age I complained about this arm hurting but no injury was visible and she was not aware of any incident where I might have broken it. As a result there was no treatment.

When the treat-it-yourself approach proved inadequate and the choice became one of seeing a doctor or an undertaker, medical advice was sought. Except for Mother, who had gone to the Mayo Clinic in Rochester, Minnesota, years before and to a rub doctor in Sioux Falls, South Dakota, somewhat later, no one in our family seemed to need the services of a doctor, but me. Not that the others didn't get sick; they did, but the liberal consumption of the grape juice that we only received when we were sick and other home treatments seemed to work for them. There were a few occasions when they did not suffice for me. Except for one occasion, I was never given shots or vaccinations.

My first known contact with a doctor was for the removal of adenoids. My sickly appearance seemed to need treatment and the departure of these growths was advised. No mention was made of the tonsils, and apparently, the ten dollar fee was insufficient to include their removal. The operation took place in the doctor's office, a room above the grocery store, with the doctor's wife giving the anesthetic. She placed the cloth over my mouth, poured on a liberal amount of ether, and told me to start counting. I did so, inhaling the obnoxious gas and counting until breathing became so difficult it appeared I would pass out due to lack of oxygen. My next recollection was one of lying on a couch in the hall outside of his office. Upon my awakening, Dad carried me to the car and we went home.

Later that night, I woke up choking on blood, which was all over the pillow and bed. Sitting up relieved the choking and reduced bleeding, so I spent most of the night sitting. The next day we went back to the doctor and he advised the taking of coagulant pills. Although bleeding continued intermittently, it was greatly reduced and healing quickly followed. More appointments with the doctor were considered unnecessary.

All of us had the usual childhood diseases and Dolores and I frequently had them at the same time, whooping it up with coughs or lying down with fevers, but only I had smallpox. My fever was such that I was incoherent much of the time, so Mother kept me in the downstairs bedroom during the day. When the seriousness of my illness became evident, a doctor was called. He diagnosed the disease and gave me a shot. I soon recovered with few pustules making their appearance.

DENTAL CARE

Toothbrushes were not unknown, but I seldom used one. Hygiene courses in school recommended daily brushing and there was a period when I did, but for the most part, if the food I ate did not remove undesirable deposits from my teeth, they remained.

I had two contacts with dentists before my entry into the service in World War II: the first was for removal of two abscessed teeth and the second for a filling and a checkup.

I was approximately ten years old when two abscessed teeth began giving me trouble. After they had oozed and ached for some time and did not heal unaided, Dad decided the services of a dentist were in order. The dentist's office was in his home, and I was encouraged to sit in a chair quite different from any I had seen. He inspected my teeth and repeated the comment all dentists must memorize on entry into dental school: "You should brush your teeth more often." He informed me that I had two abscessed teeth that had to come out. Dad agreed and the dentist grabbed a plier-shaped tool, put his knee on my chest and told me to open wide. When I did, he grasped one of the abscessed teeth with the pliers and began to twist and pull, holding me at bay with his knee—all of this without a local anesthetic. The tooth was reluctant to budge and a tug of war ensued. The dentist's eyes expressed anger and my position between him and the tooth became unbearable. I prayed the dentist would win. When pain reached an unbearable threshold, the tooth finally came out and full consciousness returned. The process was repeated on the other tooth. Although there were two gaping holes in my gums, no further treatment was required.

This introduction to dentists was not to my liking, and when I saw one the next time, years later while living at Manly, I did so reluctantly. Dad and I were in Mason City doing our periodic window-shopping when we passed a dentist's office. Dad suggested we go in and have our teeth checked, and being in a subservient position, I agreed. I insisted that he go first so the procedure could be observed from a distance and so I could have time to remove some of the excess crud from my teeth with my handkerchief. The dentist treated Dad rather kindly, stating that everything was fine, and then he looked at me with a gleam in his eye.

After glancing at my teeth, he repeated the memorized lines, changing them slightly to, "It would be nice if some day you made an acquaintance with a toothbrush." He went on to inform us that I had one small cavity and it would cost one dollar to repair. Dad agreed and out came the drill. Although local anesthetic was not used, there was no pain this time.

MOVING TO MANLY

The difficult financial conditions my parents encountered after the 1929 stock market crash ended their ownership of the Ledyard farm in 1931. They then rented the farm from the Travelers Insurance Company, who had obtained possession. This was a role they did not enjoy playing. The pride-of-ownership sales pitch that all real estate personnel must learn for entry into their field of activity had great significance for those who lived on the farm. Not only was it their workplace, but also their home and where most recreational activities took place. When driving in the country, crops, animals, farmyard, and buildings were all observed in judging the competency of the occupant. Absentee landlords were not inclined to spend money on items that did not ensure a quick and adequate return and the renter ceased to be his own boss. Owning their own farm was, therefore, the primary goal of all farmers. My parents were no exception. Since they had been renting the Ledyard farm after losing possession in 1931, their goal was to purchase a new one.

Saving money was not easy during the depression but some money was absolutely essential for the purchase of a farm. The folks had saved a few hundred dollars and they were eyeing the market for a chance to purchase when such an opportunity appeared in 1936.

Ownership of many of the farms in Iowa had been taken over by insurance companies and feelings towards them were not inclined to be good. This was well known by the elected state officials and there was some talk about restricting such companies from ownership of farms. I do not know the extent to which such legislation had proceeded or its legality from a constitutional point of view, but it was obvious to the insurance companies that this was not the proper environment for the selling of insurance and they soon made a determined effort to sell their farms back to the farmers. The Travelers Insurance Company, who owned our Ledyard farm, published a brochure listing and briefly describing all the farms they had for sale. We got a copy of this brochure and soon the looking, wishing, and planning began in earnest.

With the money they had saved and the sale of grain and animals that could be spared, it was estimated that my parents could accumulate approximately one thousand dollars, and this became a key factor in their planning. The company encouraged them to buy the Ledyard farm back, but my parents were reluctant to do this. Having purchased this farm once and lost possession, they were inclined to make their next try on a different farm in new surroundings. In any case, they made a number of trips to see other farms listed in the brochure that seemed to be potentially purchasable.

It soon became evident that a good 160-acre farm with excellent improvements and desirable location was beyond their means. They continued their pursuit, looking at an 80-acre farm near Manly in Worth County, Iowa, that had two good buildings, the barn and house, and several others quite adequate and presentable. All required painting and repair, the fences were not the best, and additional tiling would be required, but it was for sale for $5,600 and this appeared to be within their financial capabilities. Although half the size of the normal family-size farm, it appeared adequate for a minimum operation, and after extensive discussions, the folks decided to take the plunge. (It must be remembered that since they had decided not to buy the Ledyard farm, they had to move.)

The contract is no longer available, but it is known that the insurance company dropped the purchase price to $5,500 and a $550 down payment appears to have been made. This left them with a $5,000 mortgage and approximately $450 cash to make the move and set up shop at Manly. Our move to this farm became the center of our attention.

It was obvious from the beginning that this move would be quite different from the 1929 move to Ledyard; it was sixty-five miles to the Manly farm and everything had to be moved by truck. Each load would have to be carefully packed and anchored, and the number of loads required to move our household furnishings, machinery, animals, and sufficient feed for a few months would be large indeed. Friends and neighbors could offer little assistance for such a move because it was time-consuming and would extend over several months. We were on our own. Fortunately, the new owner of the Ledyard farm was going to till the land, but not live on the place or occupy its buildings, and this would permit us to move our property at leisure.

Dad purchased a used 1933 Chevrolet truck for $250 in Algona and built a twelve-foot box on top of it. The tires were reasonably good but there were no dual wheels or a spare. Since money was in short supply the purchase of these items was not considered prudent at this time. Surplus grain and animals were sold when the market appeared favorable, and all personal possessions were viewed from the standpoint of necessity and movability. A few weeks before March 1, Dad took a load of hay to Manly, but found the road in front of our farm impassable due to snow. He place the hay in a stack alongside the road near the farm and no further attempts were made to have feed available at the farm upon our arrival.

Moving day arrived and Wilbur came to help. He had hitchhiked from Dubuque to Ledyard the day before to help us get an early start. The first load into the truck contained essential household furnishings, such as the kitchen range, heating stove, beds, tables, and chairs. The car was also loaded, although its capacity was severely limited. When all was firmly in place, we proceeded down the road at a maximum speed of thirty-five miles per hour.

After moving the furnishings into the house at Manly and setting up the stoves and beds, we headed back to Ledyard for a load of milk cows. Doing chores at two locations sixty-five miles apart was not to our liking. By the time this second load had been put aboard and we were on our return journey to Manly, it was dark. This load was substantially heavier than the first and about a mile east of Buffalo Center, the right rear tire blew out. The truck was slowly driven to a farm entryway while the cows showed their displeasure at the excessive list at the rear. The truck was jacked up and the wheel removed. The movements of the disturbed cattle caused the jack to sway back and forth, leaving the stability of this arrangement in some doubt. Dad had no choice but to continue, so he took the wheel and hitchhiked back to Buffalo Center where he had a relative who operated a gas station. There he obtained two used tires and had one mounted. The relative returned him to the truck. Meanwhile, Wilbur and I were warming ourselves in the farmer's house.

Upon Dad's return, the truck was still on the jack, swaying to and fro to the beat of rhythmically inclined bovines. The wheel was replaced and substantial praying took place the rest of the way to Manly. When the cows had been unloaded, it was 4:00 A.M. and they were left unmilked until we got up at 6:00 A.M.

The two-trips-a-day schedule was maintained for several days, until the doing of chores was primarily restricted to Manly. Wilbur went back to Dubuque and I began school at Manly. There were still some animals at Ledyard and Dad made some trips on his own, but the hectic pace had abated.

It should be pointed out that the loading of large heavy machinery was challenging. Two heavy planks were used as a ramp to roll it up on the truck with the assistance of a block and tackle. Some of the equipment had to be partially disassembled and reassembled again at Manly. The picker was disassembled and never used again. Fortunately, none of us was ever seriously injured performing these activities, but there were a few occasions when this became a distinct possibility.

Our move from Ledyard ceased near the end of June. We had adjusted to life at Manly and these trips to our former home involved a certain degree of nostalgia. The unoccupied Ledyard farm seemed very lonely and isolated, and on our return, the sight of the Manly roundhouse smokestack, which could be seen for miles and which we looked for as soon as we left nearby Hanlontown, became etched in my mind as a symbol of our new hometown. A new life was beginning for us, a life with its own unique experiences.

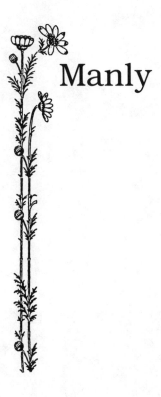

Manly

Manly house, 1945. A portion of the barn is on the left, and the oats bin is in the center background.

Manly school band, 1938. Kenneth is in the top row, third from the right, with cornet.

A Fordson tractor. This model is similar to the one we had.

Dad on the John Deere tractor, 1939. The machine shed is shown on the left and the chicken house on the right.

The Manly Farm and Community

Life at Manly began on an upbeat. Although a tremendous amount of hard work would be required, the farm's location and facilities were such that if given sufficient time and effort, it could be made into a nice homestead in a desirable setting. This farm had been a casualty of a declining economy, but a former owner had constructed a modern house, and it, with other improvements, provided a firm base on which to build. Our buoyant outlook was that better times were ahead and the small amount of money required to accomplish the task would become available.

THE FARM

As farmers became more affluent during the first few decades of the 1900s, they began replacing their typical one-and-a-half-story houses with boxlike two-story constructions that had full basements and interior plumbing. Our new house was such a structure; it contained eight rooms plus a bathroom and walk-in pantry. Since electricity was not available when this house was built, a brief explanation of its original plumbing facilities may be of interest.

A large concrete storage tank had been placed on the ground adjacent to the well with a gravity flow line to a pump in the basement of the house. This pump, periodically powered by a gasoline engine, forced water into two round, steel tanks that were approximately three feet in diameter and six feet long. The air compressed within the tank maintained water pressure for the faucets and toilet. The heating system utilized hot water and radiators. The water circulation took place by the more dense, cold water sinking to the bottom of the system while the less dense, hot water rose. A sewage septic tank and leaching tile field for disposal of its effluent was located north of the house. An underground cistern near the southwest corner of the house was used to store rainwater from the roof. This water was used for the laundry facilities in the basement. Because of the extensive subterranean limestone deposits in much of Iowa, the well water was hard, necessitating either the use of chemicals to break it for use in the laundry or rainwater that was naturally soft.

Since some of the previous occupants had not possessed pride of ownership, the facilities, particularly the plumbing, had not been maintained and all the modern conveniences were now inoperable. Although the heating pipes remained in the walls and the two large steel water tanks with accompanying pump still stood in the basement, the original heating system, including radiators, and most plumbing fixtures had been torn out. A large wash basin with drain board, where we put our water pail, was left in the kitchen, but since the septic tank was now inoperative, the drain had been disconnected and a five-gallon pail had to be placed underneath to catch the drain water. The water pipe from the tank at the well to the house had deteriorated to the point where water would no longer flow through it. The gutters and downspout on the house had rusted through, making the cistern inoperative, and its water line to the basement was also out of order. All laundry water had to be pumped from the well, hand carried to the range in the kitchen to be heated, and taken to the basement for use in the washing machine. The dirty laundry water had to be carried up the basement steps to be disposed of outside.

The condition of the plumbing did not differ from that of the rest of the house. For example, all the interior walls had been painted with a calcimine-type water base paint that had to be scrubbed off before an oil base paint could be applied. A certain degree of innate intelligence, a little money, and a lot of sweat would be needed to resurrect the house to its former glory. Such would also be the case with the other buildings on the farm.

Our small spread had been under cultivation for some time

and there was some tile in the west forty, but the natural drainage channel that ran from east to west through our farm was untiled. We did not have the problem of large ponds forming in the spring and remaining for months, as they did at Ledyard, but the crops in the low areas were to be adversely affected by temporary ponding. Extensive quack grass was in evidence and there were two thistle patches—one referred to as bull thistles and the other as Canadian thistles. Farm access from Manly was over a half mile of gravel road going north out of town and nearly one mile on an unimproved dirt road going east. A rural delivery route did not go by our farmyard and we had to place our mailbox near the road intersection at the southeast corner of our farm, approximately 300 yards away.

THE TOWN

Manly was a railroad town of approximately fifteen hundred persons, located where three different lines converged. These lines—the Rock Island, the Chicago and Northwestern (CNW), and the Minneapolis and St. Louis (M. and St. L.)—insured train activity around the clock. The Rock Island had a roundhouse at Manly where extensive repair was performed on its equipment, and this too increased activity. Except for the Doodle Bug on the M. and St. L., all engines, including switch engines, were steam powered and the wailing, moaning sound of their whistles was heard night and day. The Rock Island Rocket came into use around 1939 and its diesel engine provided a premonition of the steam engine's demise. However, until its demise, the sounds of steam engines immediately became associated with our new home; they gave us a sense of being part of a thriving, throbbing, industrial community, one that seemed larger than its physical size. The CNW track came close to the northwest corner of our farm and its trains could be clearly seen from my bedroom window; the 1:00 A.M. passenger train on this line, with its brightly lit windows, became a part of my nocturnal environment.

The town provided the usual shopping facilities and it also had a theater and a small hotel. Mason City, with a population of about twenty-five thousand, was located only ten miles south and many large purchases were made there. Its location gave us a feeling of accessibility to a large city.

Although we did not have relatives nearby, our close neighbors and our nearness to town removed the feeling of isolation we had had at Ledyard. Our loyalties were no longer split between two towns and we quickly felt a part of this community. It was friendly, somewhat more cosmopolitan, and the urban population was to exert more influence on our lives than had formerly been the case. There was no Presbyterian church in Manly, so we joined the Evangelical church, one which did not differ greatly from the Presbyterian.

Struggling against the Tide

SETTLING DOWN

We had farmed 200 acres at Lakota, 160 at Ledyard, and now we were down to 80 acres, a substantially smaller operation with a proportionally reduced income. The move had dictated the sale of a significant part of our stock and feed, the immediate effect of which was to reduce our cream and egg money. The depression had eased somewhat before our move, but deepened again in 1937 and our life-style quickly became a less than ostentatious one. Basic farm activities proceeded much as before, but there were modifications dictated by circumstances, a few of which are briefly noted below.

The grove of trees in our farmyard was a source of energy for heating, but our Fordson tractor did not have a pulley and we no longer had an adequate source of belt power so the buzz saw could not be used; Dad and I became very familiar with our two-man saw because all rounds now had to be sawed by hand. We could no longer use our grinder, but this was not a great handicap with the limited feed we now possessed. The pump jack we had used at Ledyard had worn out and been discarded with the engine, so all water now had to be pumped by hand. This task fell on my shoulders and it was one I soon detested.

Years of manure removal from the cattle barn had resulted in the dirt floor being lowered to an elevation below the ground outside, and in the spring, the water table was high enough so that the rear legs of the cows were in water. Milkers had to use boots of sufficient height to prevent this water from overtopping them and cows did not find this setting entirely to their liking either. Raising the floor seemed desirable. We accomplished this by using a team and single-box wagon to obtain dirt from alongside the road ditch next to the fence where it could be obtained without disturbing the topsoil in our field. Later, we used old railroad ties to make floors in the cow barn and horse stalls.

Apparently tenants in the past had expended all their manure removal energy on the cow barn because the elevation of this material at the rear of the horse stalls was such that the horses' rear ends were in danger of contacting the floor of the haymow above. We found it difficult to harness horses in this position and because our horses were soon adding to this elevation, the removal of this manure was commenced as soon as field conditions permitted. The old manure spreader we had previously used at Ledyard had been junked during our move, so we had to not only pitch the manure onto a single-wagon box, we also had to pitch it off. Undesirable as the conditions may have been when using the spreader, the current method was even more distasteful.

Feed was in very short supply that spring. The chickens were free to roam and had to survive on the bugs, worms, and plants they could find, a condition not conducive to good egg production. Our small permanent pasture was insufficient for our hungry grazers and it was necessary for me to occasionally herd the cattle alongside our road.

Although field operations continued much as they had at Ledyard, we now had only four horses, which limited their use in such operations. Four horses were still used on the drag, which was a task quickly performed, and three on the oats binder, but their use in other field operations was restricted to only those requiring one team. The gang plow, sulky, eight-foot disk, and two-row cultivator were never used again, and use of Dad's single-row cultivator was restricted to the garden. All plowing and disking was done by using the Fordson tractor and our corn was cultivated using my single-row cultivator. Our fate now lay in the hands of our well-used Fordson tractor.

THE FORDSON TRACTOR

Although the Fordson had its own unique deficiencies, some of which will be noted shortly, it represented the next step up from the Hart Parr in the evolutionary development of tractors. The four-cylinder engine was lubricated by a crankcase splash system that returned the oil for reuse. The clutch was incorporated with an enclosed flywheel, and power was transmitted to the rear wheels through rear axles, which eliminated the need for exposed gears. The machine and its controls were reduced in size, making it somewhat more manageable but still very much a tractor. It was patterned after the Model T and its appearance and operation were much the same: it used a similar magneto (some later models had different and more accessible magnetos), the four coils in wooden boxes were located on the dash, the ignition and gas levers were under the steering wheel, and its method of cooling and cranking was the same. Besides the engine size, which was somewhat larger, the major difference was the addition of a water-filled air cleaner and a gasoline starting tank. In one respect it was somewhat more primitive than the Hart Parr because it could be purchased without a governor (and therefore without a pulley) and ours was such a model.

The magneto was rather weak so it was necessary to spin the crank to start the tractor. Its compression left something to be desired, and starting it was not always easy to do. We soon reduced this fatiguing task by starting it with the use of dry cell batteries. After doing so, it was necessary to switch the wire back to the magneto, which had to be done with our fingers while the engine was running. The voltage put out by this magneto is unknown, but it was sufficient to cause me to perform a most undignified dance. Consequently, I always looked forward to starting this machine with some degree of apprehension.

When it started, a cloud of black smoke belched from the straight, mufflerless exhaust with a roar that could be heard for miles. Based on the experience of a Manly neighbor whose Fordson set the barn aflame with its hot exhaust gases, ours was never placed in a position where such gases could contact flammable material. After advancing the spark, adjusting the gas feed, and waiting for the machine to warm up and calm down, the fuel was switched to distillate and the driver went to sit on the throne.

The seat of the tractor was located directly over the transmission-differential housing, where the operator had to straddle it with his legs like a person riding a horse. However, unlike a horse, this unit got hot when the tractor was in operation, and the operator had to keep legs spread to avoid being burned. The exhaust pipe projected to the rear, where it conveniently terminated at a point where the full blast of its expanding gases could be appreciated by the driver, and the worm gear drive was located immediately below, where its ear-splitting, moaning sound waves were amplified by their reflection back from the ground. Since our machine was somewhat underpowered, when pulling heavy loads it would frequently slow down to the point where the clutch had to be disengaged to prevent it from stalling and the engine's roar would temporarily replace that of the worm gear.

The plow that had been purchased for use with this machine had its own peculiar traits. It had seen much use and had developed a dislike for left-hand turns, refusing to come out of the ground when one was made. This trait amplified the difficulty of operating a tractor without a governor. When such turns were required at the ends of the field, the tripping rope had to be engaged while the plow was going straight forward, a position where it generally cooperated and came out of the ground. However, it was highly undesirable to do this any farther than required from the end of the field, so judgment had to be used in this operation. When the plow came out of the ground, engine speed shot up and the gas lever had to be quickly readjusted, and while this was taking place the tractor had to be turned, which required the use of two hands. Upon completion of the turn, the trip rope was used to drop the plow into the ground and the gas lever had to be immediately readjusted to prevent the engine from stalling.

After a twelve-hour day of performing these hand maneuvers in conjunction with the footwork required to periodically depress the clutch, while at the same time making sure my legs were sufficiently spread to prevent being burned, I could not stand up. I felt like a bowlegged cowboy, dismounting from a horse with an exaggerated girth after an all-day ride. The loud ringing in my ears continued while my body maintained vibrations that had developed in harmony with the vibrations of the tractor. The machine also subjected me to other experiences of an undesirable nature.

Because they frequently failed, the bearings in the tractor's transmission had apparently been subjected to considerable stress in the past. To replace them, it was necessary to unbolt the tractor near its center and completely separate the two halves. Used bearings were purchased for approximately $2.50 from a junkyard on North Federal Avenue in Mason City, the replacement was made, and the two halves were then reunited. The last year we used this machine, which was 1938, it broke down four times and the bearing repairs became routine. I recall one occasion when I stayed home from school to plow and went to the field at an early hour. When making my first round, I noticed that the transmission lever was loose and could be pulled right out of the transmission. I managed to get the tractor back to the yard, and after disassembling it, Dad and I were on our way to the junkyard as school began.

OUR FIRST HARVEST

Our first year on the Manly farm did not prove to be a bountiful one. There was no alfalfa field or other hay land, so it was necessary for us to use what grass we could get along the road and the railroad right-of-way. Bumblebees objected to our removal of the coarse grasses on the railroad land, but we managed to get enough hay to permit our animals to survive. The reduced size of the crop permitted sufficient room in the haymow for the straw we obtained from threshing.

The cold, wet spring had proven to be ideal for our extensive quack grass, and although everything reasonable had been done to kill it, our grain crops were severely affected. When small grain harvesting time arrived we joined the neighborhood threshing ring and proceeded to participate in these activities. Unfortunately, little of it took place on our farm. It was obvious that the yield from our limited acreage would be small, but I doubt if there has ever been a case where a farmer had participated in a threshing ring and harvested a smaller crop; when threshing was completed, we had one triple-box wagonload of oats. Although the ring had a blower-type elevator that could be used to unload and elevate grain during threshing, unloading our grain that year did not require its services.

That fall, a significant part of our corn crop was cut with the binder and the rest picked by hand. Our corn crop was not even large enough to fill one tier of a temporary round snow fence crib.

Our main crop—quack grass—had to be attacked vigorously that fall to reduce its prominence the next spring. The following year would be one with severely limited animal feed with all that this implied.

HARD TIMES

As the end of 1937 approached, our financial maneuverability had declined to a point where we were locked inside an incomeless box. Our limited cream and egg money not only had to buy our necessities, but also sufficient feed to keep our animals alive. The procedure became one of using enough of this money to buy a sack or two of feed from the elevator so that our cows and chickens could produce enough cream and eggs to repeat the process. To say we were living from hand-to-mouth would be incorrect; it was more like living from feed-sack-to-feed-sack.

We could not afford to butcher one of our few steers, so that winter we made due with one hog. Mother's specialty, meatloaf, was in short supply and its substitute, eggs, were needed to obtain cash. But our garden crops were good and we became vegetarians out of necessity.

Our finances finally deteriorated to the point where my parents could not make the one hundred dollar a year principal payment on their loan, and payment of taxes was deferred and interest payments delayed. It wasn't long before a Travelers Insurance Company representative came to the farm and had a long talk with Dad. The discussion ended when it was agreed that the principal payment could be deferred, but interest payments had to be made. This temporarily removed the threat of foreclosure proceedings.

How the money was obtained, I do not know, but the payments agreed to were made. It was during this period that Dad attempted to borrow one hundred dollars from the bank and was unable to do so. Suffice it to say this was not done without its emotional cost. Bitterness appears with the disappearance of hope and those who find themselves in dire financial straits too often give up the fight. Fortunately this was not the case with my parents.

Since our survival on the farm was in doubt, income had to

be increased and much thought was given to various means of doing so. Our acreage was too small to obtain sufficient funds from the sale of grain and our hog and beef operations could not be expanded without more feed sources. The maintenance of a somewhat larger and more efficient dairy herd appeared more feasible. Acquiring such a herd would require the production of sufficient grazing plants and fodder, and the acquisition of cows that were better adapted to transforming the feed into butterfat. There were few choices, and this became our course of action.

The purchase of good dairy cows required money we did not have, and the money could not be obtained from the bank. Fortunately, government organizations had been established to assist farmers in making such purchases and Dad borrowed two hundred dollars from the U.S. Production Credit Association in Mason City. A purebred Guernsey cow was purchased from a dairy west of that city. Expansion of this nucleus was intended in the future; meanwhile, our less productive shorthorns would continue their contribution to the cause.

Because our permanent bluegrass pasture was inadequate, we tried other crops to supplement our grazing needs. Sudan grass was used as a temporary pasture and also for hay. Rape was grown one year and used as a pasture, and soybeans, now becoming a significant cash crop, were also used as hay by cutting the plant before the bean ripened and the plant died.

Good quality fodder could be obtained for a dairy herd from corn plants that were cut before maturity and ensiled in a container that prevented their contact with oxygen, and the usual means for doing so was by use of a silo. Since there appeared to be no way to acquire such a structure, consideration was given to the use of a trench silo (simply a hole in the ground where ensilage could be placed and covered over to reduce its contact with air), until we heard that a wood stave silo had been disassembled and was going to be disposed of on a farm near Manly. This appeared to be the opportunity we were looking for, so it was purchased for a few dollars and we used the truck to haul the parts to our farm. The construction of a concrete foundation and the erection of a structure quite different from our others began.

The lumberyard at Manly had forms for making a circular concrete foundation for such a structure, and they could be borrowed at no cost if the cement was purchased from them. The forms were brought to our farm, an inner and outer circle was formed with a twelve-inch space between them, and the inner circle was wired to the outer circle for support. Limited reinforcing was available but a steel rod or two was used. Concrete was mixed in our usual manner: a shallow wooden box was constructed on the ground, seven shovels of gravel and one of cement were placed in the box, and a hoe was used to mix them. When thoroughly mixed, water was carried in a bucket and added until the right slump was obtained. Buckets of concrete were emptied between the forms.

The wood superstructure consisted of one vertical row of hatchways (they were removed from the top down as silage was removed) within a vertical framework, and staves in two different lengths bound together by steel hoop rods tightened around them like the steel bands around a wood barrel. One long and one short stave provided the thirty-foot height, with the length of adjacent staves alternated. The hatchway frame and all staves had to be in place before the hoop rods could be put about them and tightened in order to provide a stable structure. We had never seen such a structure erected and had no special equipment to do so, but with sufficient effort, we were confident that we could accomplish the task.

We began early on a day when there was little or no wind. The hatchway frame was put in place and temporarily supported horizontally by boards nailed to the barn located a few feet away. Staves were put in place starting on each side of this frame, temporarily attaching them to the frame and then to each other by nailing 1″ × 4″ × 4″ wood blocks across the joint between them. The staves, extending thirty feet in the air, received some support from each other as they began to curve around the circular foundation, but not much; it was necessary to place the top stave by using a ladder that leaned against the previously placed staves while one of us braced the inside of the silo. Construction of this wobbly structure continued throughout a long day until closure was finally made. Fortunately, the wind remained calm. We could not leave the structure overnight without all staves and at least a few bands in place, which we finally succeeded in accomplishing.

The next day, the rest of the bands were put in place and all properly tensioned. When this procedure had been completed, the diameter of the structure was somewhat less than we had anticipated and the staves were located dangerously close to the inside of the concrete foundation. We had to add concrete on the inside of the foundation to increase its width, and upon its completion, we had a silo. I eagerly anticipated my first silo-filling experience.

In a fashion similar to threshing rings, farmers who had silos worked together to fill them. We joined our neighbors in this activity. The corn was cut with the corn binder immediately before silo filling and was not shocked. The bundles of green corn were substantially heavier than small grain bundles and could not easily be handled with a fork, so one side of the hayrack was removed and the bundles picked up from the ground by hand and placed on the rack. At the silo, they were removed from the rack by hand and thrown into the feeder of the ensilage cutter, which was powered by a belt from a tractor. The bundles were cut and shredded into small pieces and a blower elevated them up and over the top of the silo. I found this bundle hauling to be the most physically taxing of any task on the farm, especially when sorghum was grown with the corn. Bundles then approached a hundred pounds in weight.

The production of silage involves anaerobic fermentation that imparts a distinctive taste to the fodder, a taste the cattle seem to like. However, when air is permitted to participate in the curing, the fodder simply spoils and the moldy result has to be discarded. Since the ensilage at the top of the silo was exposed to air, spoilage of a foot or two there was normal. Because the joints between the staves of our silo were not air tight, we experienced additional spoilage around the perimeter. As a result, this source of fodder was not as efficient as it should have been, but we still had reason to believe it was better than the use of corn bundles in which the ears, leaves, stocks, and husk had been dried like hay. Unfortunately, spoilage was not to be the only source of trouble with the use of this structure.

After the silo was empty in the spring, we gave it no further thought— until one summer evening while we were milking. A rainstorm had approached and strong gusts of wind were soon evident, but this was not unusual. All of a sudden, an extra strong gust hit the silo and it collapsed with a crash. We dashed outside to see a large pile of tangled debris. Some of the rods had been badly bent, a portion of the hatchway frame had been damaged and some of the staves had splintered.

Substantial effort was required in untangling the mess and stacking the undamaged parts for reassembly. The structure was erected again, but only to a twenty-foot height—the length of the longer staves. This erection went somewhat faster but with less enthusiasm. All circumferential rods were thoroughly tightened and the superstructure was anchored to the foundation with cables.

Its existence in an abbreviated form also proved to be a short one. It was used during the winter of 1939–1940, but in the spring of 1940 another windstorm sealed its fate. It blew down again and this time it stayed down. Dad later used the longer staves as roof joists for a lean-to he constructed against the north side of the barn.

While we were experiencing trouble with the silo, obstacles were being encountered in the expansion of our dairy herd. More purebred cows could not be purchased and we did not have the means to have our cows artificially inseminated. As a result, our bull, not being a purebred Guernsey, diluted the strain of our Guernsey's offspring and our dairy herd remained primarily shorthorn in nature, with a diminishing strain of Guernsey embedded within. Although the production of butterfat increased slightly due to the introduction of this strain, it did not prove to be sufficient to materially increase our income. Times would remain hard.

Of course the silo was not the only structure demanding attention; a certain degree of repair and maintenance was required to insure the integrity of all our buildings. Painting was a task now actively pursued. Red lead paint was low priced so this was the paint used on all buildings except the house and pump house. It was purchased in five-gallon cans. It took thirteen gallons to give the barn one coat. The exterior of the house was painted white, and this color was also used as trim on the other buildings. The entire interior of the house was painted by the women after all the whitewash-type paint had been removed.

THE JOHN DEERE TRACTOR

After our experiences with the Fordson during the spring of 1938, it was obvious that we had to get a better tractor or get out of the farming business. Here again money was the problem. That fall and winter Dad and I frequently looked at used tractors and we finally found one that was acceptable and priced low. It was a row crop Model B John Deere, a two-bottom plow size. It came with a detachable two-row cultivator and was for sale at the John Deere dealer in Mason City. It had been originally sold with steel wheels and later the owner had purchased rubber tires and kept the rear steel wheels. The dealer had it for sale for $475 with the rubber tires or $425 with steel. This was the tractor we wanted. The problem was how to buy it.

Although rubber tires were preferred, financial considerations eliminated them and bargaining began for the tractor equipped with steel wheels and detachable cultivator. After an extensive bargaining session, the dealer agreed to take the Fordson—sight unseen—on a trade for $50 credit and the deal was closed with the $375 balance to be paid in time payments. We now had a dependable tractor, and field operations could be planned with some degree of assurance that they could be carried out. These operations were now to enter a new phase, one in which horses were to play a smaller and smaller role.

The two-cylinder engine used in the Model D John Deere had proven to be popular and reliable, and the Models A and B utilized this same type engine with its exposed flywheel and hand-operated clutch incorporated in the pulley. The engine was started by turning the flywheel by hand. The typical "tu-cut" sound of the engine was now somewhat dampened by the vertical exhaust system and the steering mechanism operated easier than our car or truck. It had zerk grease fittings and a foot brake for each rear wheel, which could be locked in place for belt work or to assist in making sharp turns. Our tractor had fenders, even though most were purchased without.

When plowing with nonrow crop tractors, the right wheels rode in the previously made exposed furrow and this tended to guide the front wheels, but the front wheel(s) of row crop tractors could not do this and steering, although much easier, became a full-time job. If properly positioned for cultivating, the rear wheels were somewhat too far apart for the right rear wheels to ride in this furrow when plowing, at least with our two-bottom plow. John Deere tractors had long rear axles, which meant the wheels could be moved in and out, permitting adjustment to the operator's preference. When mounting the cultivator, we had to move them out, and when plowing, they were moved in.

The steel seat on this tractor permitted movement in the vertical direction only and traveling over rough ground was not a pleasant experience. However, provisions were made for standing and the controls were such that this was easy to do. When disking plowed ground the first time, standing was the position generally assumed.

We continued to use our horses for planting corn, raking hay, and pulling wagons, but the tractor was taking over more and more of their duties. Cultivation was rapidly performed and I drove the tractor while Dad operated the oats binder. The corn binder was pulled by the tractor with the bundle carrier down, which meant that bundles were dropped at random and not in windrows, so an operator was not required. This tractor also gave us a source of belt power and the grinder and buzz saw were now back in use; although with less power, greater caution was needed in feeding them. The tractor was too small for the shredder, but this was of little consequence. Dad kept this tractor until his death in 1954. By then he had had the lugged rims burned off the rear wheels and rims for tires added. This eliminated the need for horses and they were disposed of.

The Manly Public School

The Manly Public School was primarily a city school with a few farms immediately surrounding the town part of the district. The brick structure was somewhat larger than Ledyard's, but the condition of its interior indicated an earlier beginning. Other differences were a larger, more cosmopolitan student body, including a few blacks, no bus service so that walking to school was now a part of the routine, overalls not commonly worn to school at any age, and a football team as well as the usual baseball and basketball teams.

THE NEW ENVIRONMENT

On entry, the city influence and more formal attire was immediately apparent. Fortunately, I was wearing corduroy trousers that I had acquired when I started high school. There were so few boys from the farm in high school that we ate our lunch in a small area of the basement that had been cleared for storage, and the gymnasium was not made available for our use. (The girls from the rural areas ate lunch in the home economics room, and those who lived in town went home for lunch.) I had some concern that acceptance on the part of the majority would be difficult, but all seemed friendly and there was no overt discrimination.

Classroom and band activities were tougher. My academic abilities were quickly put to the test. The first day in algebra class we were given a quiz in factoring, something unfamiliar to me, and I received an F. Memories of my failures at Ledyard now returned. Fortunately, I found adjustment to the other classes easier. A few days later, I eagerly carried my cornet to school and received another disappointment; the band director checked my playing ability and said it was insufficient for me to be a member of the concert band.

Although my entry was somewhat rocky, the more urban setting was intriguing and that stimulated my interest. I never proved to be a brilliant student, but I did manage to pass all my subjects. Because my chances of going to college were practically nil, my interests were directed at what appeared to be a more suitable career—farming.

VOCATIONAL AGRICULTURE CLASSES

Although the number of students from the farm was small, the school participated in the teaching of vocational agriculture under a program supported in part by the federal government's Smith-Hughes Act of 1917. Courses extended over three years, one year each for farm crops, animal husbandry, and farm management. A few of the boys from town joined those of us from the farm to form an adequately sized and enthusiastic class, and vocational agriculture was to be part of my curriculum from my sophomore through my senior year.

The classes, and related activities, proved to be educationally broadening beyond the scope of agriculture. All aspects were of interest, including the public speaking and, of course, the field trips. Short trips were made to nearby farms to observe the latest techniques in tasks somewhat familiar to me, such as castration, and longer field trips were made to observe some unfamiliar farm related procedures. A few of these come to mind.

The north side of Mason City had two industrial plants that we observed every time we went to the city on Highway 65. During certain times of the year, the sugar beet plant emitted a highly undesirable odor over an extensive area surrounding the plant. The other plant was a cement manufacturer that spewed material into the atmosphere of such a nature that nearby houses were painted a cement-colored grey. A field trip to these industrial giants exposed me to a working environment not to my liking.

At the cement plant, I saw workers operate machines that bagged cement. This task involved taking an empty sack, attaching it to a machine, operating a control to fill the sack, lifting the sack, and setting it aside with others. This procedure was performed in a mechanical, robotlike manner, over and over throughout the day with a more than desirable amount of cement always escaping into the surrounding air.

Although the air in the beet plant appeared somewhat cleaner than that in the cement plant, its odor-polluting ability was unchallenged. No doubt workers soon became accustomed to it, finding fresh air rather strange, but otherwise the factory environment appeared very similar to the environment of the cement plant.

On one occasion, we made a one-day trip to the twin cities, Minneapolis and St. Paul, to go through a packing plant, a newspaper office, and to the top of the Foshay Tower. In the packing plant, hogs were led through a small passageway to a large wheel, where their rear feet were attached to a chain that went up over the wheel, taking the screaming hog with it and hanging it upside down. The hog was slowly conveyed through the sticking room where the sticker, standing silently and with very little apparent movement, stuck the hog in the throat, cutting its jugular vein as it slowly moved by, and the blood gushed from the animal as it continued to scream and foam at the mouth. The floor was covered with coagulating blood, making it necessary for the sticker to wear boots. As the conveyer chain continued to move slowly along, the hog quickly weakened and its frantic cries diminished in volume until they ceased. When the chain moved the animal from this room, it was dead, and as it proceeded slowly along, workmen stationed along its pathway performed various operations on the carcass. Its removal from this chain did not take place until it was in the cooler. Later, after the body heat had dissipated the carcass was taken to another area where it was cut up and packaged. Although assembly line activities were in evidence, these procedures did not seem to differ greatly from those we used at home.

The cattle operation did not appear as dramatic. They were hit in the head and knocked out before the coup de grace of sticking took place. Extensive, emotional bellowing was not in evidence. The workers in both operations performed their specific tasks rapidly and in what appeared to be an effortless, efficient manner.

When our tour of the packing plant was over we went to a newspaper office. With my extremely limited writing experiences, it seemed that the effort required to write the numerous articles in a daily newspaper was a gargantuan one, and the setting up of complicated machinery, the rapid printing process, and the packaging of countless newspapers was an eye opener. The environment was much more pleasant than the packing plant, but other conditions appeared much the same. After this visit, I viewed newspapers with more respect.

Our tour ended with an elevator ride to the top of the Foshay Tower. Although this structure is now dwarfed by adjacent high rises, to us it was a skyscraper and the view from its top unsurpassed. I wondered how workmen could build a structure so high in the air because the view, looking down while working on the outside, would surely discourage them from doing so.

Some of our trips were of a more social and recreational nature. Our instructors were graduates of Iowa State College (now Iowa State University) at Ames and close liaison was maintained with activities at this school. One spring we attended VEISHEA, camping out on the campus during our visit.

Since the instructor and/or affluent parents always furnished automobile transportation, my only expense during these excursions was the purchase of food and necessary entrance fees, which I could manage, but there was one formal two-day affair that proved to be beyond my means. As a member of this class, I joined the Future Farmers of America (FFA) and one year I was chosen as one of the delegates from our chapter to attend the convention held in Des Moines.

Transportation was to be furnished, as usual, but we were told to take along five dollars for hotel, eating, and other expenses, for which we would be reimbursed later. Dad questioned me long and hard on this point and finally agreed to lend me the five dollars with the understanding he would get it all back upon my return. Since this would be my first experience at staying in a hotel and attending such an event, I looked forward to it with pleasure.

The hotel was an old downtown structure where we were assigned three to a room. There was a wash basin in the room but the bathroom was down the hall. Our view overlooked a rear courtyard and an adjacent wing of the hotel. Ostentatious it was not, but the experience was a unique one for me.

The most memorable part of the convention was the last

event, a banquet attended by the governor of Iowa. The contents of his speech have faded from memory, but the formality and size of the group in attendance has not. Its significance to the growing of corn or the raising of hogs somehow escaped me.

Upon our return, we made a report to our chapter of the proceedings, and we were reimbursed $3.50 apiece for our expenses. Unfortunately for me, my expenses had been nearly $4.00. I recall no riotous living on my part, but this was no consolation for Dad. He was furious at me for either misinforming him as to the expenses to be reimbursed or for my spending more than necessary. This considerably dampened my interest in attending such events in the future.

My agriculture class activities were for the most part pleasant, but one was not, and it was for me especially enlightening. We have a tendency to be unaware of or ignore actions of an undesirable nature if they don't negatively affect us, and such was the case with me as far as racial discrimination was concerned. Although I had heard of its existence, it did not appear to be a problem in our community because I was not a recipient. There were a few black students in our school and one, Alfonso Douglas, was in my grade and agriculture class. The blacks lived in their own area near the roundhouse and had their own Baptist church, where Alfonso was a deacon. As a result, he was naturally called "Deacon," or "Deac" for short.

One year, as members of this class, Deac, Eldon Hungerford, and I attended the Dairy Cattle Congress in Waterloo. When noon arrived, we went into a small eating establishment to get something to eat. I was looking at the menu as we sat in a booth and not paying any attention to the waitress when she said something to Deac. He and Eldon immediately got up to leave and I, not knowing what had transpired, proceeded to follow. I asked why they were leaving, but Deac would not answer. Eldon stated that they would not serve Deac. This confused me, but I said nothing.

We proceeded to look for another place and finally went into a diner establishment and sat at the counter with Deac between us. The waitress asked me if he was with us and I said yes, and she answered, "In that case, he can stay." Finally, it dawned on me that if I were black and alone, finding a place to eat could prove difficult.

After this experience, I became aware of other racially discriminating practices taking place: the Glee Club in which Dolores sang had a black girl who was not permitted to participate in some of their contests with other schools, social gatherings were not mixed affairs, and on one occasion a student jokingly told Deac he could not go crow hunting with us that night because he might get shot. At no time do I recall Deac complaining. He was one of our team's best football players and in all class activities he was accepted as an equal and as a friend. On other occasions, he was seldom seen.

BAND

Dolores and Anna Marie played the piano, but not competitively in contests, and neither was interested in playing an instrument in the school band. Although I was a member of the church choir for a short period of time, singing held little interest for me, but the band interested me to a great extent. However, there were two hurdles I had to surmount before I could become a member: I had to have a pair of white trousers and my playing ability had to meet minimum standards.

Fortunately, Mother found a pair of white trousers Wilbur had discarded and this problem was quickly solved. The school furnished the cap and coat necessary to complete the uniform. A solution to my playing ability was more complex. Although I practiced at home, I doubt if my ability had improved significantly, but eventually the band director put me in the cornet section of the concert band—I sat in the last chair. I did not see my expertise in this activity improving and I gave serious thought to abandoning it. However, these activities, and the camaraderie with other members, all of whom lived in town, appealed to me and I decided to make my limited, unique contribution—at least for awhile.

The band was not only involved in school events and Saturday night concerts in the Manly park, but it also participated in various contests and in the annual North Iowa Band Festivals at Mason City. All of these events interested me, but I was especially drawn to the national contests and the North Iowa Band Festival. The year that I was a member, the band competed in the National Regional Music Contest that was held in Minneapolis. All competing bands were required to play a Rossini overture, *The Barber of*

Seville, a Bach chorale, *Jesu, Joy of Man's Desiring,* and an unknown selection for sightreading that was given to the band at the contest a few minutes before it was to be played. In preparing for this event, we had band practice before school began and during the last hour of the day. We played the two known selections over and over until they became so much a part of us that even now, fifty years later, they remind me of this organization and this event.

The trip to Minneapolis was a one-day affair that was made by car. Our part in the contest was quickly over and we won second place.

The North Iowa Band Festival was an annual spring event held in Mason City shortly after school was over. Concerts were given in the bandstand in Central Park, marching bands participated in a parade, and a mass band concert was held in the evening. This event introduced me to marching band activities, and since displaying our abilities under such circumstances brings out the vanity in us all, I proudly strutted along with the rest, showing off my uniform, but being careful about displaying my musical ability.

Although I did not appreciate my position, I enjoyed being a member of the band. Two of the members were good friends of mine and no one discriminated against me for being from the farm. However, it was apparent that my position in the organization would not improve, and I ceased participation after a year. I had learned and experienced much and it would not be forgotten, but further participation offered little for me or for the others.

SPORTS

My interest in sports had also greatly diminished due in part to my inability to see games because I did not have the money required for entrance fees. I saw one basketball game at Manly, but no baseball or football games. I did make an attempt to see a football game.

Since Ledyard had no football team and the games we played during the noon hour were unsupervised and highly irregular, I wanted to see the game played as it should be. When my friends heard of this, they said, "No problem, just go with us in the car and lie on the floor in back under our legs and the ticket taker will never see you." I agreed and off we went to the football field west of town. To my dismay, the principal was taking tickets. He immediately spotted me and looked rather angry, but said nothing. I quickly removed myself from the car and walked home. I made no further attempt to see a football game at Manly and avoided the sport until I was in college.

A Teen Faces the Future

SOLITARY PURSUITS

Upon our move to Manly, the Fada radio was put in the attic and never used again. However, Wilbur brought us a beautiful console battery-operated radio that he had purchased in Dubuque. An explanation of its acquisition may be of interest.

Farms were now becoming electrified, and as they were, farmers bought radios and other accessories that used 110-volt AC. (Some farmers had installed a 35-volt home-plant system that used a gasoline engine or wind-powered generator. The wiring for these systems was too small for the 100-volt system and had to be replaced when connected to a power line.) Apparently, some traded in their battery-operated sets, and since the market for these radios was rapidly diminishing, they were offered for resale for just a few dollars. The set Wilbur obtained cost $2.50, and it had such modern features as single-dial program selection, bass-treble tone control, and shortwave, police, and marine band frequencies, as well as the usual AM. Its fidelity was much greater than that of the Fada and musical programs were a delight to listen to. Unfortunately, it required batteries and as a result its use was generally restricted to that of being a nice piece of furniture, enhancing a corner of the living room.

My activities at school exposed me to the availability of a crystal detector set for eighty-nine cents, and it appeared to offer real possibilities because no batteries were required for its operation. Earphones had to be used, but we still had our Airline Special headset, so this was no problem. Mason City had obtained its first radio station (KGLO) a short time before and its antenna appeared to be within range. I could see the red warning lights on its quarter wave-length Marconi antenna from my bedroom window at night. I decided to proceed, and I scraped up enough money to order the set.

Upon receiving it, I installed an antenna wire from the dormer of the house to a tree, oriented as per directions, and we were ready for cost-free radio.

The discomfort resulting from the small, hard earpieces pressing firmly against our ears did not increase its popularity, so family competition for its use was never in evidence. However, the radio did provide some diversion for me, and Dad got the news from it. It proved to be my last contact with radio before leaving the farm.

CAR MAINTENANCE AND REPAIR

Dad now took less interest in machine maintenance and I was more on my own with such matters. The grouchy, temperamental Fordson tractor was not my only patient; our 1931 Chevrolet also needed my attention. In addition to the usual brake lining, clutch, and bearing replacements, a few less conventional ones come to mind.

One of the most aggravating weaknesses of this vehicle was its rear axles. Metallurgy had not yet progressed to the point where fatigue failures were unknown in these components and they would progressively develop cracks through their diameter, eventually breaking without warning. We referred to this as crystallization since the break had a crystalline appearance. On one occasion it happened when I had the car in Manly for the evening. The resulting response was typical—a short walk home, towing the car home the next day with a team and wagon, ordering a new axle from the catalog, and waiting to receive it to make repairs. This repair became so routine that Dad constructed a special tool to extract the piece of axle remaining in the differential without having to remove the differential cover and the grease.

The hard use and somewhat less than professional care the car was being subjected to were not entirely to its liking, so all the engine's internal organs eventually needed to be replaced. We went to the junkyard to negotiate for an engine replacement. They had several well-used, six-cylinder Chevrolet engines that fit our car, and for ten dollars, we could have our choice. They all appeared the same, so we chose one, loaded it up on our trailer, and headed for home.

The car was placed under an adequate tree limb where a block and tackle could be used for hoisting, and work commenced. When the job was done, we started the car to see what we had purchased. The engine sounded better than our old one, which may have been due, in part, to our imagination because we were earnestly hoping to reap some benefits from this investment. It was to suffice until the car's demise several years later.

GETTING MY DRIVER'S LICENSE

I did not get a driver's license as soon as age permitted me to do so. There were several reasons for this: an inadequate vehicle to drive for the driver's test, insufficient funds to pay the fees, and last but not least, little enthusiasm on Dad's part to provide me the means to take the car further than Manly on my infrequent nights out. He did not have money to buy gas for excursions of a frivolous nature and this was, no doubt, a convenient means of applying restraint. Eventually, I reached the age where lacking a license became a source of embarrassment, and then an all-out effort was made to get the money. We eventually did so, and it was up to me to make the car legal for the inspection.

Repairs had to be made without cost and most were easily accomplished. However, the horn button operation remained erratic and the brake light was only operative about 60 percent of the time, not a good performance record for a vehicle about to be inspected, but we decided to proceed.

I took the test at the old courthouse located north of Central Park in Mason City. After completing the written portion, I approached the driving test and vehicle inspection with some degree of apprehension. The horn was no problem since I could continue to manipulate the button until it worked, but when the officer asked me to press the foot brake to see if the brake light worked, I kept my eye on him to see if there was an immediate response; if not, I was prepared to move the pedal back and forth vigorously until there was. He made no comment, so apparently the laws of probability responded in my favor. I took him for a ride while I manipulated the steering wheel, with its excessive play, in a fashion not unlike that of a helmsman operating the wheel on a ship.

FRIENDS

A natural separation seemed to exist between those who lived in town and those from the farm; the selection of pals and buddies seemed to be pretty much confined to those who lived in the same environment that you did. However, my participation in the band, where there were no farm youths, also resulted in a few friends from this group. Most of the activities with my farm friends have been briefly noted, but those with my town friends differed somewhat.

The Eighteenth Amendment to the Constitution (1919) prevented the sale of alcohol to the general public. It was repealed by the Twenty-first Amendment in 1933, and retail sales were then controlled by the states. Iowa had chosen to limit acquisition of bottles to state-operated liquor stores and beer was the only alcoholic beverage obtainable in bars. Manly possessed such facilities but my friends and I were not old enough to go there legally. However, this did not prove to be an insurmountable barrier. There were those among my town friends who had older cooperative friends who were not above doing them an occasional favor, and the consumption of alcohol soon became the means of expressing Manly behavior.

Beer was the usual beverage consumed under these circumstances, and it was to be my first contact with the strong stuff. Its taste was not to my liking, so the amount I drank proved to be insufficient to favorably impress those of my peers who were inclined to admire this activity.

During Prohibition, stories about the availability of bootleg liquor were common, but I soon discovered that reports of its demise at the hands of the Twenty-first Amendment were somewhat exaggerated. My second contact with alcohol took place when a friend of mine discovered that this product could be obtained from a place in the northern part of Mason City, and the thought of obtaining it in manner that was socially frowned upon enticed us into trying. A car was driven to the front of the establishment, where a member of our group went to the door with the money and handed it to someone through a partially opened door while telling the recipient what he wanted. He was told to go to the back of the building, where he was handed a package through another partially opened door.

Our package contained one-half pint of pure alcohol, firewater much too strong to drink straight, so we poured a small amount from a Coke bottle and replaced it with alcohol. After some degree of mixing, we were ready to enjoy a frontier-style cocktail.

Although we didn't admit it, I suspect that the taste was to no one's liking since our consumption of this drink was extremely limited. Having proved a rather dubious point, the evening's festivities ended with an appreciable amount of firewater left. The individual showing the most interest took the bottle and buried it in the lawn near his house where he could retrieve it later.

It should be noted that some dancing establishments had facilities that made it easy to mix drinks. Drawers were located under the table tops of the booths where you could place your bottle and conveniently, but discreetly, put the proper amount in soft drinks ordered from the establishment.

Dating was not to occupy a significant part of my activities while in high school; the number of dates I had could be counted with the fingers on one hand. My romantic pursuits had to await another day, another time, and different circumstances. No doubt there were those sufficiently endowed with a pleasing personality to pursue this game, even with handicaps such as mine, but fate had not seen fit to number me among them. However, curiosity did lead me to observe romantic activities of a public nature.

The school did not have dances, but there was a dance hall located at the intersection of the two highways at Manly and an after hours place located near the roundhouse, where such activities could be pursued after the dance hall closed. There was also the Surf Ballroom at Clear Lake, twenty miles away, for those who wanted to go to a high-class affair where name bands frequently played.

I had no one available to teach me how to dance. However, a friend of mine knew of a club in Mason City where dancing was taught and they gave a free lesson to all prospective customers.

We went and were given our free lesson, which proved to be of dubious value to me. I recall only one other occasion where I attempted to navigate about a dance floor with a female partner and my performance was not outstanding. I was used to handling bundles of grain while shocking oats, but the close embrace of a girl while attempting intricate maneuvers with my feet was beyond my capabilities. I soon found my natural niche on the sidelines as an observer, and I soon developed a great proficiency for observing at the dance hall in Manly.

Here dances were held every Saturday night during the summer and many rural young people, as well as a few urbanites, participated with gusto. The one-story barnlike structure did not have booths, but benches were located around its perimeter, and along each side were shutter openings conveniently placed at the right height for observers to watch while standing outside. It cost nothing to watch, and having nothing else to do, I spent a great deal of time observing others dancing. The consumption of courage-inducing liquids was not unknown and males occasionally became involved in activities of a more physical nature. An adequately sized bouncer was a necessity.

This dance hall closed at 1:00 A.M., but those who wanted to extend the evening went to an establishment near the roundhouse. I was told that here they could continue dancing and drinking until dawn, and I suspect many did. Although not an active participant, there were a few occasions when I observed the inside of this place of amusement. Nonpaying guests were not encouraged to remain and my visits were of brief duration.

If a young man wanted to really impress his date, he took her to the Surf at Clear Lake. Such an evening could cost as much as five dollars, an astronomical sum that prevented most from participating, and those who did, went infrequently. Although I later had a glimpse or two of the inside of this facility, I rarely went there.

CHURCH ACTIVITIES

The comments above could well lead anyone to believe that my church activities had ceased, but such was not the case. As previously noted, we attended the Evangelical church and here I ushered, passed the collection plate, sang in the choir, and occasionally went to rallies at nearby churches on Sundays. Social activities were sometimes held in the church basement, and I also recall an ice skating party. Our pastor, the Rev. Henry Raeker, was to provide the means for me to pursue my education after high school.

DEPARTURE FROM THE FARM

During my senior year, I gave much thought to my future. I was not particularly interested in farming because it involved extensive, hard physical labor with little financial reward and my ability to engage in it appeared limited. Our eighty-acre farm was too small for two male adults and renting more land did not appear feasible. Even if extensive acreage could be rented, our limited equipment made its cultivation difficult. A hired hand's future was not a bright one and this role I rejected immediately.

My tours through industrial plants had convinced me that a blue-collar job in town should not become a part of my future; many farm tasks required great physical labor, were tedious and boring, and not a few were performed in clouds of dust, but surely man's destiny was meant to be more profound than that of a robot, performing repetitious tasks in a mechanical manner under rigidly controlled time schedules and constant supervision. However, sitting at a desk all day long, day after day, doing tedious white-collar work did not appeal to me either. Additional education appeared to be the only means of attaining what would be a more pleasant way of making a living. However, additional education posed problems: there were no colleges within commuting distance that taught courses I was interested in and no funds were available to go to one that did.

I had heard that there was financial assistance available for needy students attending Iowa State College at Ames, so I convinced Dad to permit me to hitchhike to Ames to get the details. On campus, I found no one who encouraged me to believe entry could be made with no money at all, although financial assistance might be obtained after I became enrolled. It was apparent that for the present at least, this school was beyond my reach. The college helped me get a fifty-cent room for the night in the city, and I returned the next day.

I was not the only one seeking further educational opportunities and our desires did not go unnoticed. Our pastor, Rev.
Raeker, took several of us in his car on a one-day trip to visit
Western Union College in Le Mars, Iowa, an Evangelical church
college at the time. (The name was changed to Westmar in 1948
and to Teikyo-Westmar University in 1990.) Although it was
small, one could take preengineering courses or pursue a teaching career. The school offered employment opportunities for its
students not only in such school activities as waiting on tables,
janitorial services, and assisting teachers, but also in such
diverse areas as making venetian blinds, raising vegetables on
empty lots in town, canning vegetables, and working on farms.
There was still, of course, the question of entry. Could I enter
such an institution with literally no money at all?

I had no funds and after our return, Rev. Raeker contacted
the school to see if Donald Chlupach and I could work during the
summer and have our earnings credited to our account when we
enrolled in the fall. The school officials agreed and within a few
days after I graduated from high school, Don and I hitchhiked the
175 miles to Le Mars and began working for twenty-one cents an
hour—credit, not cash—plus board and room. Rev. Raeker had
opened the door of opportunity; now it was up to us.

The wheels of destiny were rolling slowly forward to an uncertain rendezvous, not only for us but for those who chose to till
the soil. The family farm was in transition; it was shaking off the
last vestiges of the draft horse, and fortunately, was about to enter a new and brighter era. All that we are does not cease to be
just because our surroundings change; substantial time was to
pass before chore time each evening did not bring back thoughts
of those tasks that had become so much a part of my life. Like a
horse trained to pull fire-fighting vehicles, when the bells started
to ring, I began to chafe at the bit. It is indeed true, as frequently
stated, that "you can take the boy off the farm but you can't take
the farm out of the boy." For this, I make no apology.

Epilogue

Although prices were frozen during much of World War II, economic conditions improved for my parents during the early 1940s due in large part to increased production. I had obtained samples of hybrid seed corn in the spring of 1940 from Iowa State College through my agriculture class, and the yields that fall from this seed convinced Dad to use it exclusively. A phone was installed in 1945, connection was made to a power line in 1946, and the farm mortgage was paid off. Money saved during the war was used to purchase, among other things, more modern machinery.

Dad died in May of 1954 and Mother soon sold the farm and moved back to Kamrar. My direct tie to the farm was completely severed.

For those who define success only in terms of dollars and cents, my parents proved to be only modestly successful. However, for those of us who knew them as a deeply concerned father and mother who placed greater emphasis on the quality of life obtained through mental stimulation, they could not have been more so.

The physical features of all the farms and communities I have written about now differ substantially. The school that had existed adjacent to our farmyard at Lakota disappeared many years ago. The farm site is occupied, but the buildings there now were all constructed after 1929.

A few years after we moved from the Ledyard farm, new buildings were constructed and the site was again occupied. Later, these buildings were removed and the ground now exists

217

without evidence of previous habitation by man or beast; the former ponds are now shallow, lifeless depressions. The modern school building at Ledyard has been abandoned and the town now buses its children to an adjacent community. The railroad that served Ledyard no longer exists.

Of the structures that existed on the Manly farm when we lived there, only the house and corncrib remain. The house, two appurtenant structures, and several acres are now a separate piece of property and are occupied by a nonfarming family. The rest of the farm and the corncrib are now owned by the Hungerford family.

Train activity at Manly has been drastically reduced. When diesels replaced steam locomotives, the roundhouse was no longer needed and maintenance activities ceased. Its chimney was removed years ago and what remains of the roundhouse is now used as a granary. The railroad we used to walk along is gone and the creamery adjacent to it is an abandoned ruin. The depot and the two-story structure where the numerous rail switches were manually operated are also gone. Although a gym that was constructed later is still there, the school we attended has disappeared, and a new regional high school exists east of town.

The true significance of these changes is apparent in retrospect. There is a feeling of timeless infinity, of insignificance, of sadness when viewing a place where once we worked, played, laughed, and cried, and finding that the hardships and pain we bore have left no trace. However, change is an essential ingredient for the maintenance of hope; without it, life would cease to be worth living.

In recent years, it has become popular to refer to the disappearing family farm in a regretful nostalgic manner, but I am not sure that the image this projects is a correct one. If it is Grant Wood's pitchfork-in-hand farmer, its demise took place years ago. If it is a diversified farm operation, limited to one family living off the land by raising its own vegetables and meat and growing its own seed, such operations have not been a significant part of Iowa farming for decades. If it is an operator-owned business where pride of ownership is the primary ingredient, this too now exists only on a limited basis because renters now till a substantial portion of the land in some of our most agriculturally oriented states. If it is the highly touted rural environment, supposedly beneficial for the raising of children, why do so many rural landowners rent their land and live in an urban environment?

Perhaps what is implied is agribusiness with a degree of family participation. Regardless of definition, operations on the farm now differ substantially from those that existed in the 1920s. It could not be otherwise, nor in the final analysis would any of us want it to be.